Key Stage 3

THE MAKING OF THE UK

Mark Hubbard

Roger Knill

Philip Allan Updates
Market Place
Deddington
Oxfordshire
OX15 0SE

Orders
Bookpoint Ltd, 130 Milton Park, Abingdon, Oxfordshire, OX14 4SB
tel: 01235 827720
fax: 01235 400454
e-mail: uk.orders@bookpoint.co.uk
Lines are open 9.00 a.m.–5.00 p.m., Monday to Saturday, with a 24-hour message answering service. You can also order through the Philip Allan Updates website: www.philipallan.co.uk

© Philip Allan Updates 2007

ISBN 978-1-84489-428-4

All rights reserved; no part of this publication may be reproduced, stored in a retrieval system, or transmitted, in any form or by any means, electronic, mechanical, photocopying, recording or otherwise without either the prior written permission of Philip Allan Updates or a licence permitting restricted copying in the United Kingdom issued by the Copyright Licensing Agency Ltd, 90 Tottenham Court Road, London W1T 4LP.

All efforts have been made to trace copyright on items used.
The illustration on pp. 30–31 was done by Bob Moulder.
Other illustrations are reproduced by permission of: Bristol City Museum and Art Gallery, UK/Woburn Abbey, Bedfordshire, UK/Harris Museum and Art Gallery, Preston, Lancashire, UK/The Crown Estate/Bridgeman Art Library (pp. 2, 8, 10, 19, 34–35, 38, 61); Angelo Hornak/Corbis (p. 57); Dover Publications (background artwork throughout and illustration on p. 74); Ingram (p. 54); Mary Evans Picture Library (pp. 62, 66, 67, 73); The Sealed Knot (p. 32); TopFoto (pp. 4, 6, 7, 9, 12, 13, 14, 17, 22–23, 24, 27, 28, 40, 41, 42, 43, 44, 45, 46, 48, 50, 52, 53, 58, 59, 60, 61, 64, 70, 71, 72, 74).

Design by Neil Fozzard.

Printed in Great Britain by CPI Bath.

Environmental information
Philip Allan Updates' policy is to use papers that are natural, renewable and recyclable products and made from wood grown in sustainable forests. The logging and manufacturing processes are expected to conform to the environmental regulations of the country of origin.

Contents

Topic 1 Why was religion so important? 2

Topic 2 How hard was it to keep England Protestant? 12

Topic 3 Did Charles I throw away the crown of England? 24

Topic 4 Did kings have to obey the laws of their land? 40

Topic 5 Was Cromwell really just another king? 48

Topic 6 How powerful were kings and queens? 58

Topic 7 Was England cursed by evil? 62

Topic 8 Were plague and fire a disaster for London? 66

Topic 9 Was there a revolution in England, 1500–1750? 76

Topic 1
Why was religion so important?

How dangerous was it to be a heretic?

Source A — What is going on in this picture?

Starter activity

Look at **Source A**. What would you most like to know about it to help you understand it? Write down at least five questions you would like to ask about the image (e.g. Who? Where? Why? What? When?)

The gruesome picture above (**Source A**) shows two people being punished for their religious beliefs. The two men are being burned at the stake.

This was a common punishment for religious **heretics**. Heretics were people who did not share the same Christian beliefs as their monarch.

Heretics were burned because people thought that the flames would cleanse away their sins. The two men in Source A were important religious figures. One is Nicholas Ridley, the Bishop of London. The other is Hugh Latimer, a **Protestant** preacher. Why would anyone want to burn religious leaders?

The Catholic Church

The Queen of England at the time of the burnings was **Mary Tudor (1553–58)**. She was the eldest daughter of Henry VIII. Mary was a **Catholic**. This meant that she followed the teachings of the Catholic Church and the leadership of the Pope in Rome.

The Pope had been at the centre of some problems for previous English monarchs. Archbishop Thomas Becket died as a result of Henry II's quarrel with the Pope in 1171.

Martyrs

Religious strife was nothing new in England, but in the sixteenth century it had become a major problem. Latimer and Ridley became famous martyrs for their faith. They were believers in a new branch of the Christian Church, **Protestantism**.

Martin Luther

In 1517, in Wittenburg in Germany, Martin Luther nailed a list of his complaints about the Catholic Church to the door of his local church. These complaints, or protests, became the basis of the new ideas. His followers became known as 'Protestants'. It was to be a momentous change.

Source B: The main differences between Catholic and Protestant beliefs

Catholic beliefs	Protestant beliefs
The Pope is the ruler of the Church.	Jesus is the real leader of the Christian Church. He has no representative on Earth.
The priest is the only person who can carry out a service.	People do not need a priest to help them pray.
The service or Mass must be in Latin.	Services and the Bible should be in English so that everyone can understand them.
The Bible must be in Latin.	
Churches should be highly decorated with many statues, paintings, music and the smell of incense. The altar should be the most decorated part of a church.	Churches should be plain and simple so that people concentrate on worshipping God only.
Priests must not marry.	Ministers should be ordinary people who dress simply.
People should confess their sins to their priest in church.	Ministers should be allowed to marry.
If you give gifts to your church this will help you get into heaven.	God is the only person who can forgive sins.
If you go to church you will go to heaven.	
If you don't worship correctly, you will go to hell.	If you don't worship correctly, you will go to hell.

Activity

1. Which do you think are the most important differences between the two faiths described in **Source B**?
2. Why do you think people were so afraid of going against the established Church?
3. How dangerous was it to be a Protestant if the monarch was a Catholic? Explain your answer carefully.

Topic 1   Why was religion so important?

Did Henry VIII plunge England into chaos?

Starter activity

Look at the portrait of Henry VIII. What clues are there that he was a powerful man?

Hint: look at the way he is standing, his clothes and jewellery, his expression.

Henry VIII became King of England in 1509. He married Katherine of Aragon (a Spanish princess), who had been married to his older brother, Arthur. Arthur had died tragically young in 1502.

Like Katherine, Henry was a good Catholic. The Pope had even given Henry a special title, 'Defender of the Faith', to show that he respected him.

Henry and Katherine had a daughter, Mary, in 1516, but Henry wanted a son to take over from him. Despite Katherine being pregnant a further 16 times, no boys survived as **heirs** to the throne.

The idea of a divorce

By 1526 Katherine was worn out by the pregnancies and was too old to try for children any longer. Henry thought that God was punishing him for marrying his dead brother's wife.

Henry VIII: the image of power

Henry believed that England had to have a king to **succeed** him on the throne. For this to happen, he would have to change his wife. In 1527, Henry asked his Chancellor, Thomas Wolsey, to ask the Pope for a divorce.

The Pope said no. Wolsey was terrified of telling Henry the decision. He died on his way to London — many people thought that he was literally scared to death.

Henry was not happy with the answer from Rome. He asked two other advisers what he should do. Thomas Cromwell, a lawyer, told him to break away from the Catholic Church. Thomas Cranmer, a priest, also supported this idea.

The break with Rome

In 1533 Henry took the decision to break away from the Catholic Church and changed the rules. He passed the Act of Supremacy, which made him the 'Supreme Head of the Church of England'.

He had split with Rome and now did not have to ask the Pope to grant his divorce. His new Archbishop, Thomas Cranmer, agreed to the divorce. His new Chancellor, Thomas Cromwell, also approved.

For others the change would not be so easy to accept.

Activity

1. No picture is painted without a reason. You have already identified some points about Henry from his portrait, but what can you infer about the painting itself?
   a Who wanted the portrait painted?
   b What was the purpose or message of the portrait?
   c Who was meant to see it?

2. Draw a storyboard like the one below to continue the story, using the text for information. You cannot use words, only initials and numbers.
   a Draw enough pictures to show the key points under the headings 'The idea of a divorce' and 'The break with Rome'.
   b Lightly shade any two causes for the king's actions in green and any two effects of his actions in blue.

3. Why might Cranmer and Cromwell have been keen to advise the king to split with Rome?

4. Which groups of people in England might not have welcomed the sudden change of religion?

Henry and Katherine: a storyboard

Topic 1   Why was religion so important?

How far were Henry's motives selfish?

When people make a decision to do something, they always have a reason. We call these reasons **motives**.

Henry's decision to change the English Church from Catholicism to Protestantism in 1533 was a huge one. He was changing not just his own religion, but that of his subjects as well. Many people believed this change was a big mistake. They might be worshipping in the wrong way, and might go to hell — for ever.

Why would Henry make such a change? Why would he risk so much?

Did Henry change the Church because he fell in love with Anne Boleyn?

Thinking aloud

The reasons why we do things help to explain our actions. When people plan a holiday they consider many factors, some of which may be related (e.g. distance and cost). Major events in history often occur as a result of many different reasons, some of which may be more important than others. Deciding which are the important reasons as opposed to the lesser ones is a vital skill. Recognising that some reasons are linked helps us to gain a deeper understanding of why events happened as they did.

Activity

① Look at the possible reasons 1–12 for Henry wanting to change the religion of England.

Henry did it all for England's security ←——————————————→ Henry did it all for his own good

Copy the diagram above into your exercise book and decide where each reason should go on the opinion line. For example, if you think Henry wanted to change the Church when he fell in love with Anne Boleyn (reason 6) because he was selfish, write the statement or its number closer to the end of the line where you have written 'Henry did it all for his own good'.

② Many of the reasons why Henry split with Rome were linked. Write a paragraph explaining how.

Henry wanted to change the Church because…

1 He wanted a male heir.

2 He wanted to divorce his Catholic wife, Katherine of Aragon.

3 Katherine of Aragon was from Spain, a very Catholic country.

4 He could make himself the head of the Church of England.

5 He resented the power and influence of the Pope.

6 He fell in love with Anne Boleyn.

7 Anne Boleyn was pregnant, possibly with a son.

8 The Archbishop of Canterbury could be forced to marry Henry and Anne.

9 He could gain control of all the churchmen in England.

10 He was bankrupt after fighting so many wars abroad.

11 He resented the wealth and power of the Church.

12 He resented the wealth of the monasteries.

Henry VIII

Topic 1 Why was religion so important?

Did Henry gain at all?

The dissolution of a nunnery

Henry VIII faced major difficulties in breaking away from the Catholic Church, but he also gained a lot. He was now the leader of the new Protestant 'Church of England'.

Divorce

Henry was able to gain a divorce from Katherine, but without the Pope's permission. This enabled him to marry his new love, Anne Boleyn, who was pregnant with his child.

Wealth

Henry also began to gain wealth as a result of closing down the monasteries of England. His excuse was that the monks should live a more religious life.

He sold off Church lands to wealthy people and confiscated the gold and silver from the churches and monasteries. The 'new' churches were supposed to be simpler and plainer so that people could concentrate on worshipping God.

The **dissolution of the monasteries** gave Henry useful extra income.

The Pilgrimage of Grace

The problems came in 1536, when Henry's plans for dissolution were in full swing. His closure of 800 monasteries led to 10,000 monks and nuns being made homeless. This sparked a revolt in the north, led by a lawyer from Yorkshire called Robert Aske. Aske agreed to lead the rebels as long as the protest was peaceful. He called it a 'Pilgrimage of Grace'.

The rebels carried religious **icons** of the Catholic Church, pictures and bread and wine for the Mass. They demanded that Henry stop the dissolution, and gained the support of some nobles. For example, Lord Darcy disliked the 'commoner' Thomas Cromwell and the religious changes that people thought he had encouraged.

The rebels took over York, so Henry had to act. He sent troops north to quell the rising of about 30,000 rebels. Despite his obvious fury (Henry was well-known for his temper) he instructed his troops not to attack the rebels. Instead, Henry offered them all a pardon for their **treason**. He even told them that he would rethink his policy on the closure of the monasteries.

The rebels went home, but Henry unleashed a severe backlash. Two hundred of the 'pilgrims' were executed as rebels.

The Pilgrimage of Grace

Activity

1. Draw a simple pair of scales in your exercise book. Leave enough space to write above each side of the scales.
   a. Think of as many advantages (positive effects) and disadvantages (negative effects) as you can of Henry's decision to change to the Protestant religion. Write the advantages on the left side of the scales and the disadvantages on the right side.
   b. Colour the advantages and disadvantages **red** for very important, **orange** for fairly important and **green** for not very important.
   c. Decide whether there were more advantages or disadvantages to the change by comparing the numbers and colours of the effects. Write a paragraph explaining your answer.

2. Look at the story of the Pilgrimage of Grace. Imagine that you are making it into a television documentary.
   a. Think of a title that will make people want to watch the documentary. It could be a provocative question about Henry's motives or a dramatic statement about what he did.
   b. Make a list of the important facts that the viewer will need to know by the end of the programme.

Topic 1 Why was religion so important?

Changing times, changing religion

Source A

An Elizabethan punishment

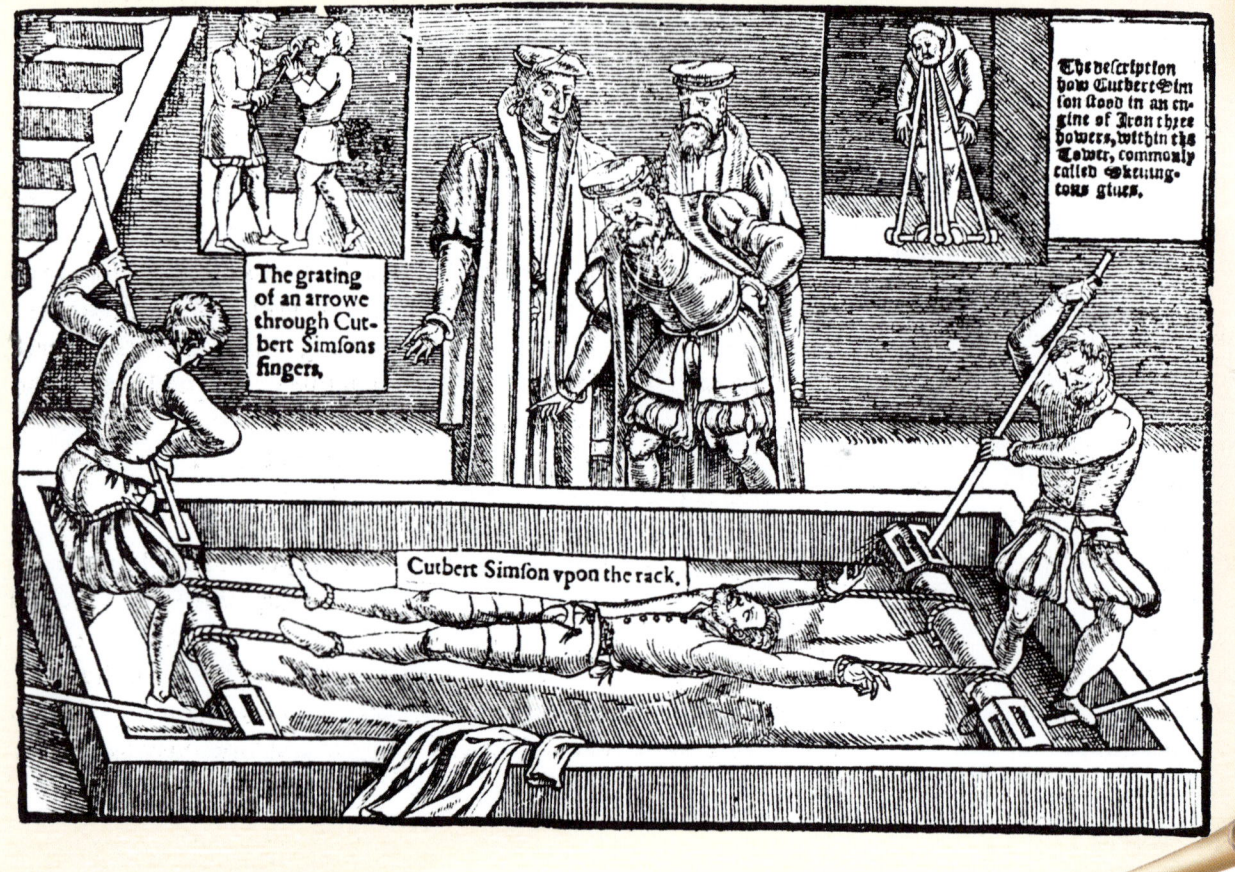

Edward VI

Henry VIII had two daughters and a son. **Edward VI** ruled after his father's death, for 6 years (1547–53). He was the youngest of Henry's children and was only 15 years old when he died in 1553. His mother was Jane Seymour, Henry's third wife.

Edward altered the Church much more than his father did. He changed all the services and the prayer books to English, and allowed priests to marry.

He also stripped all the pictures, statues and other decorations out of the churches. They were unrecognisable from how they had been earlier.

The Church became very Protestant.

Source B: How Catholics and Protestants disagreed

Problem	Catholic attitude	Protestant attitude
Who should be the head of the Church in England?	Only the Pope can be the head of the Church.	The monarch must be the head of the Church of England.
Who should deliver the service in church?	The priest is the only person who can deliver Mass.	There should be no special priests with expensive robes, but someone should read the Bible to the congregation.
What language should the service be in?	Latin is the only correct language for the Catholic Mass.	It has to be in English, otherwise no one will understand it.
How should the churches be decorated?	They must have pictures and statues of saints, to focus people's prayers.	They should have no idols to distract people from their prayers.
Should people have to go to church?	People who do not go to church will not go to heaven. Those who do go should also do good things for others.	People do not have to go to church as long as they have a belief in Jesus Christ.
Should priests be able to marry?	No	Yes, if they want to.
Should the Church be more Catholic or more Protestant?	There is only one true faith, the Catholic faith.	There is only one true faith, the Protestant faith.

Mary Tudor

You have already seen what happened to Protestants when Edward's elder sister **Mary** became the queen in 1553 (page 2). As the daughter of Katherine of Aragon, Henry's first wife, she was a staunch Catholic. She married Philip II of Spain in 1554 and became even more determined to be a strong Catholic monarch.

Mary burned Protestants at the stake. She also swept away Edward's changes, and forced priests and their wives to separate. She banned the English prayer book and made all services Latin again. She even reinstated the Pope as the head of the Church in England.

Elizabeth I

By the time Mary's younger sister, **Elizabeth**, became queen in 1558, the tensions between the two religious groups were getting worse. Elizabeth was the daughter of Anne Boleyn, the woman for whom Henry had changed the religion of England.

Not surprisingly, Elizabeth was brought up as a Protestant. By the time she became queen, the pendulum of religion had swung both ways. This did not make England easy to govern.

Activity

1. Imagine you are an adviser to Queen Elizabeth I, who has to help solve her problems. Elizabeth has to bring peace between Catholics and Protestants, so she needs to find a middle way, but she is a Protestant, and has to show that she is in charge. Look at the table in **Source B**. What solution would you suggest to Elizabeth for each problem?

   Draw a table in your exercise book with two columns, headed 'Problem' and 'My solution'. Copy the problems listed in Source B into the first column and write your solutions in the second.

2. Look at **Source A**. It shows a man being tortured on a rack in 1563. Do you think it was more dangerous to be a Catholic or a Protestant during the reign of Elizabeth I? Give as many reasons as you can to explain your view.

Topic 2
How hard was it to keep England Protestant?

How big a threat was Mary Queen of Scots?

Starter activity

Look at the portrait of Mary Queen of Scots. What symbols in the painting indicate that she is a powerful woman?

Choose five words to describe her from the following list:

regal	wealthy	desperate	beautiful
young	old	scheming	confident
determined		powerful	religious

Give at least one reason for each of the words you have chosen.

Mary Queen of Scots

The strength of Elizabeth's rule

Elizabeth I realised what she had to do to make her reign (1558–1603) secure. In matters of religion she steered a middle course. This did not upset too many people, but she dealt harshly with **extremists** of all kinds. So she managed to keep most people happy.

The Catholic threat

However, Elizabeth's cousin, Mary Queen of Scots, created a problem for Elizabeth when she arrived in England in 1568. She was a Catholic with a claim to the throne of England. What should Elizabeth do?

Fact box

Mary's past
- Mary married Lord Darnley, who was an alcoholic.
- Darnley accused Mary, who was pregnant, of being unfaithful with her secretary, David Riccio.
- Riccio was murdered by Darnley and his friends in 1566. He was stabbed 50 times.
- Darnley was murdered in 1567. His house was blown up, and as he staggered through the gardens he was strangled.
- The chief suspect was a man named Bothwell.
- To make matters worse, Mary later married Bothwell.

Source A

What can I do about Mary?

Elizabeth I

- Send her back to Scotland, where the nobles may kill her.
- Imprison her in a castle somewhere in England.
- Allow her to stay with me at the palace at Hampton Court, and protect her from any threats.
- Name her as the next queen of England when I die.
- Build her a castle of her own to live in undisturbed, as long as she denies any claim to the English throne.
- Execute her.
- Build her a castle of her own to live in undisturbed, but make the Catholic nobles in England pay for her upkeep.
- Put her back on the throne of Scotland instead of her son, James.

Activity

You are going to advise Elizabeth on dealing with the threat from Mary. Look at the options open to Elizabeth in **Source A**.

1. Write the options out in order of most severe to least severe. Add any other solutions you can think of.

2. Read the following problems. For each one, suggest a solution from Activity 1 and explain why you think it is the most suitable. You might want to discuss your ideas with a friend.

   a. Mary Queen of Scots arrived from Scotland in 1568, a Catholic from a rival country, and the cousin of Elizabeth I. Elizabeth was trying to calm the hostility between Catholics and Protestants at the time.

   b. Mary believed herself to be the rightful heir to the throne of England, as she was the granddaughter of Henry VII.

   c. The Pope advised all English Catholics to support Mary's claim to the English throne (in 1570).

   d. Mary had many secret supporters among the English nobility.

   e. A number of foreign monarchs were supporters of Mary, particularly the Catholic Philip II of Spain, whom Mary had named as her heir.

   f. In 1570, Elizabeth's chief minister, Sir Francis Walsingham, set up a spy network. He claimed to have found evidence of numerous Catholic plots to get rid of Elizabeth and make Mary the queen. However, there was very little hard evidence to prove it.

   g. Parliament was terrified that there were Catholic plots to get rid of Elizabeth and make England Catholic again. It even feared foreign invasion.

   h. In September 1586, Anthony Babbington plotted with six other Catholic nobles to kill Elizabeth and place Mary on the throne. Babbington wrote to Mary explaining his plan, but the letter was intercepted by Walsingham.

   i. Walsingham and Elizabeth allowed Mary to receive the letter. She replied to it, agreeing with the plan. Mary was ready to let a rebellion put her on the throne of England.

3. Which solution did you use most, and why?

4. Why was it so difficult for Elizabeth to decide what should happen to Mary?

Topic 2 How hard was it to keep England Protestant?

Did Mary's death solve the Catholic threat?

Starter activity

Many people wanted Mary dead. The imaginary newspaper article in **Source A** shows the kind of persuasive arguments that they used. How has the writer tried to convince the reader to agree with this view?

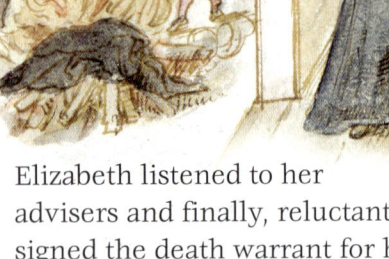

Elizabeth listened to her advisers and finally, reluctantly signed the death warrant for her cousin. In the 19 years that Mary lived in England, they never met.

Mary's execution

Mary Queen of Scots was executed in February 1587 at Fotheringay Castle. The axe struck two blows. When her head was held aloft, her wig fell off, revealing a greying, older woman. Her faithful dog crept out from beneath her skirts, and lay down at her side.

Mary was gone, but the problem of Catholics for the English monarchy was far from over.

Source A

What persuasive language has been used here?

Tudor Times

Last week it was proved beyond all doubt that Mary Stewart, the former Queen of Scots, has been plotting yet again against the life of our dear queen, Elizabeth. It is clearly difficult for our beloved monarch to consent to her own cousin's death. Yet after 19 years of threat and betrayal, surely the time has come to sign Mary's death warrant?

Source B

Mary's last letter

Royal brother, having by God's will, for my sins I think, thrown myself into the power of the Queen my cousin, at whose hands I have suffered much for almost twenty years, I have finally been condemned to death by her and her Estates....

Tonight, after dinner, I have been advised of my sentence: I am to be executed like a criminal at eight in the morning. I have not had time to give you a full account of everything that has happened, but if you will listen to my doctor and my other unfortunate servants, you will learn the truth, and how, thanks be to God, I scorn death and vow that I meet it innocent of any crime, even if I were their subject. The Catholic faith and the assertion of my God-given right to the English crown are the two issues on which I am condemned, and yet I am not allowed to say that it is for the Catholic religion that I die, but for fear of interference with theirs....

...by having prayers offered to God for a queen who has borne the title Most Christian, and who dies a Catholic, stripped of all her possessions....Give instructions, if it please you, that for my soul's sake part of what you owe me should be paid, and that for the sake of Jesus Christ, to whom I shall pray for you tomorrow as I die, I be left enough to found a memorial mass and give the customary alms.

Wednesday, at two in the morning

Your most loving and most true sister

Mary R

Activity

1. You are going to put yourself in Elizabeth's place. Write a letter to your subjects to explain why Mary was executed and to convince other Catholics not to rebel. You must also show Protestants that you are a strong monarch. Use the Skill box to help you.

2. Part of the last letter Mary wrote (to the King of France) is shown in **Source B**.
   a What evidence is there that the long confinement and trial did not change her views?
   b Do you think her execution caused the Catholics in England to:
   * renounce their faith?
   * practise their faith even more secretly?
   * seek revenge?

Skill box

Persuasive writing involves trying to make a case for a particular point of view and convincing the reader you are right.
You need to:
* Explain your point of view clearly to the reader.
* Give a number of reasons for your actions and examples of what you have done for each point you make.
* Use connecting phrases such as 'because of this...' and 'as a result, this meant...'. This will help your writing move logically from point to point and prove why you are right.
* Use persuasive language. Phrases such as 'the real reason is...' and 'you have to agree that' make what you say sound believable; phrases such as 'beyond all doubt' and 'clearly' make it sound definite.

Topic 2 How hard was it to keep England Protestant?

Was the Armada really a great English victory?

Mary's execution led to some Catholic countries becoming suspicious of the growing power of Protestant England. The Catholic King of Spain, **Philip II**, was particularly angry at the news.

Philip was already annoyed with England because English pirates often robbed Spanish ships of their gold and Sir Francis Drake had attacked Cadiz in 1587. Philip therefore determined to attack and defeat England.

Spanish preparations

Philip needed time to gather equipment and 130 ships. Recruiting an army of 30,000 troops and finding someone to lead the **Armada** also needed time. The journey itself would be difficult if the weather was not in the Spaniards' favour.

The admiral of the Spanish navy died suddenly, and the fleet was led instead by the Duke of Medina Sidonia. He was not a skilled sailor, he suffered from seasickness, and he was reluctant to take part in the Armada.

The Armada sets out

The Armada first set out in April 1588, but a huge storm blew the fleet off course.

It had to return to port in Spain, having lost many of its supplies. Some people saw this as an omen that such an attack should not be carried out.

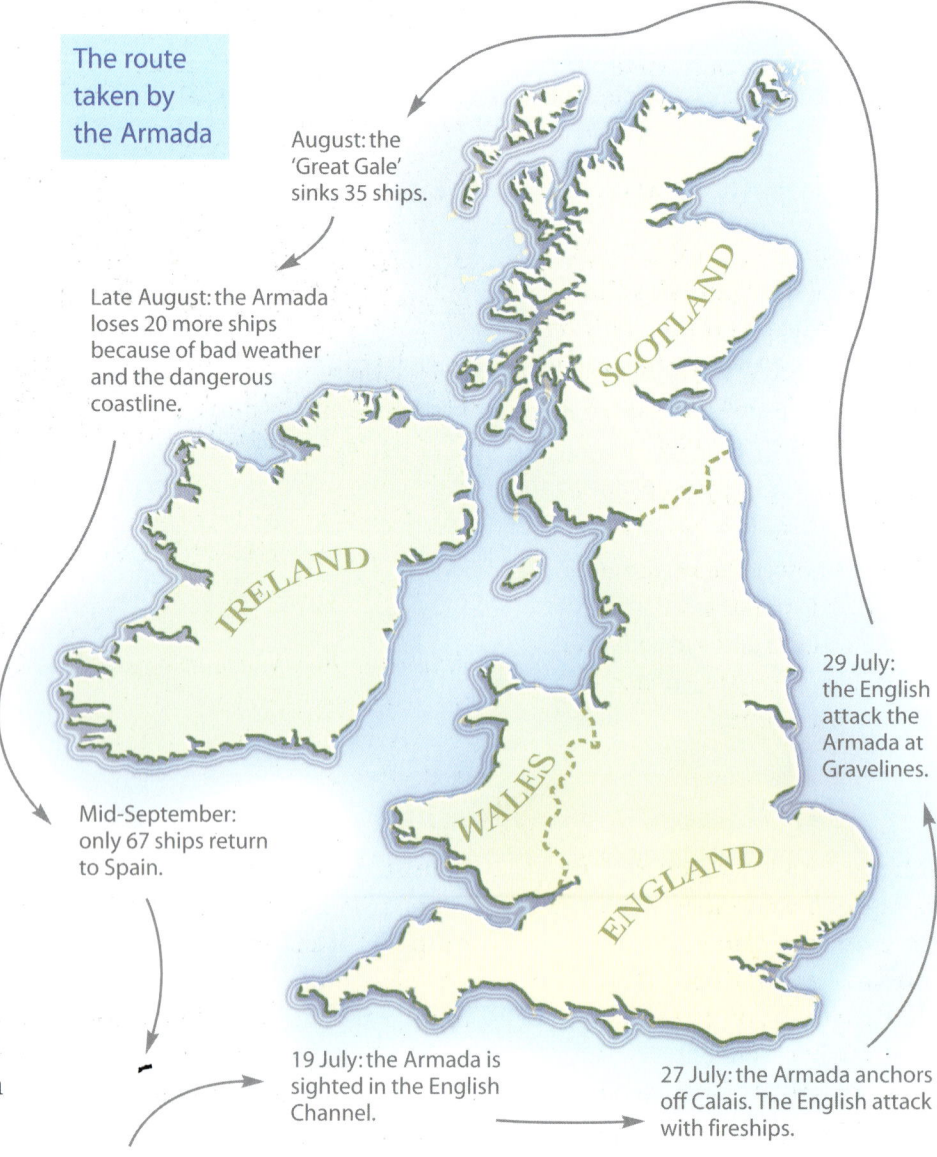

The route taken by the Armada

August: the 'Great Gale' sinks 35 ships.

Late August: the Armada loses 20 more ships because of bad weather and the dangerous coastline.

29 July: the English attack the Armada at Gravelines.

Mid-September: only 67 ships return to Spain.

19 July: the Armada is sighted in the English Channel.

27 July: the Armada anchors off Calais. The English attack with fireships.

By July 1588, the great fleet of fighting ships was ready again. The plan was for the fleet to sail up the English Channel to Calais, in France, where it would meet up with the Spanish army in the Netherlands, led by the Duke of Parma. The ships of the Armada, loaded with these troops, would then sail up the River Thames and launch their attack.

By 19 July the Armada had arrived in the English Channel. It was an impressive sight. Painted red and yellow, the ships were in a defensive **crescent-shaped** formation.

English preparations

When 'spotters' on the English coast saw the Spanish ships, they lit beacons on the cliff tops to alert everyone to the danger. An army of 5,000 men was raised to defend London.

Lord Howard and Sir Francis Drake led the 28 ships of the English navy. These were helped by much smaller vessels, such as fishing boats. Together they gave chase to the Spanish fleet.

The battle

The two fleets skirmished for 6 days. The Spanish lost three ships before finding safe harbour at Calais on 27 July. The first part of their plan had worked. They were to wait for the Duke of Parma's 30,000 troops from the Spanish Netherlands. But the troops never arrived, because they were delayed by fighting in the Netherlands.

The English attacked the Spanish fleet at anchor off Calais — using 'fireships'. They stuffed gunpowder and brushwood into eight ships and set them alight, then cut them loose from their moorings and let the tide and wind take them to the Armada.

The Spanish were terrified when they saw the fireships and decided to put to sea. They couldn't wait for their army. One Spanish ship was sunk in the panic.

The Armada was split up, and without the protection of the crescent shape the ships were more vulnerable. The English ships attacked on 29 July and fought for another 6 days. The Spanish lost four more ships and several others were badly damaged. They had to sail on. The attack on England had failed.

The Spanish Armada

Activity

Identify at least three potential problems that could affect the Armada's plans.

Topic 2   How hard was it to keep England Protestant?

The disaster

It was now a question of getting home safely. The Spanish had to sail up the east coast of England, round Scotland and out to the west of Ireland, through dangerous seas. It was a journey they had not planned for. Supplies were low and many sailors starved to death.

At least 35 Spanish ships were lost in a storm. Another 20 were shipwrecked in the treacherous waters off the west coast of Ireland. By September only 67 ships had made it back to Spain.

The English fleet did not lose a single ship, although approximately 50 sailors died — far fewer than the 1,000 or so dead Spanish sailors.

Philip's attempt to invade Elizabeth's Protestant stronghold had failed, and he would never attempt it again. Elizabeth had a medal struck for her navy which read 'God blew and they were scattered'.

Causes of the defeat

The results of battles are often recorded as the victors report them, claiming glory. However, historians agree that the defeat of the Armada probably had many causes. A major problem for the Spanish fleet was the bad weather. Philip II remarked, 'I sent you to fight men, not the weather'. There were also other significant reasons for the defeat. For example:

- The Duke of Medina Sidonia was reluctant to take command of the Armada.
- The plan had failed once already because of bad weather, and no alternative plan had been made.
- The English galleons had more artillery to fire at the Spanish ships. The Spanish were more concerned with transporting troops over to London to fight.
- The beacons gave advance warning around the coast of England so that people could prepare for the attack. The element of surprise was lost.
- The Spanish could not get fresh supplies easily, while the English fought close to home.
- Philip was not able to influence his sailors once they had left port.

Activity

1. Look back at the account of the Armada and its route. The following numbers can all be found in the text and help to tell the story. Write down what each number refers to.

   a 6   b 50   c 8   d 67   e 30,000
   f 20   g 3   h 5,000   i 1,000   j 35
   k 4   l 0   m 130

2. How many ships belonging to the opposition did each side sink by its own actions?

3. Write a script about the Spanish Armada for a 4-minute radio broadcast on the BBC news, to celebrate the anniversary of its defeat. What facts will you need? Your report should explain the reasons why the Armada was unsuccessful as well as telling the story. Before you write your script, think about the part each of the following played in the defeat:

   beacons   fishing boats   the navy   fireships
   Queen Elizabeth I   Philip II of Spain   the Duke of Medina Sidonia

4. Imagine your report has to be rewritten for Spanish radio. Which parts of the story will you emphasise for the defeated nation and which will you play down?

5. Read the final section of text, 'Causes of the defeat', and review your report on the Armada. In the light of these new facts, are there any parts of either version that you would change? How far was this a great English victory?

A portrait of Queen Elizabeth I after the Armada

Overview activity

1 Look at the portrait of Elizabeth. Find the following things in the painting:
- a a crown
- b jewellery
- c a globe
- d the Spanish fleet before battle
- e the defeated Spanish fleet
- f a mermaid

2 There is a symbolic reason for each of these features of the picture. What do you think each one means?

3 Why do you think Elizabeth wanted to be painted sitting, with a stern expression on her face?

4 Elizabeth made an impassioned speech to her troops when the threat of invasion was at its worst:

'I know that I have the body of a weak and feeble woman, but I have the heart and stomach of a King, and of a King of England too.'

Suggest what the victory meant for:
- a the popularity of Elizabeth
- b the position of England in the world
- c the religious uncertainty in England

Topic 2 How hard was it to keep England Protestant?

Gunpowder, treason… but whose plot?

Why do we burn an effigy of a man on a bonfire and let off fireworks on 5 November every year? By the end of this section you should be able to explain.

Elizabeth's death in 1603 left a problem for England. The Virgin Queen never married and so left no heir to the throne. Given all the problems that we have seen so far, this was another chance for religion to divide the country.

James VI of Scotland and I of England

The person who became the new king was the only one with a real claim to the throne. His name was **James Stuart**. He was already the King of Scotland, where he was known as James VI. James was the son of Mary Queen of Scots, but unlike his mother, he was not a Catholic. Hopefully, he could bring calm to what was a potentially explosive situation.

James and the Catholics

The Catholics thought James would relax the harsh laws that made it difficult for them to worship. Instead, he continued to make life difficult for them. Some Catholic nobles soon began to think that the only way to improve their lives would be to change the religion of England once more.

To do this, they would blow up the king and parliament, and put a Catholic back in control. This is known as the Gunpowder Plot, and the traditional story is as follows.

The plot

A group of angry young Catholics met at the Dog and Duck pub in London in April 1604. Their leader, Robert Catesby, had a plan to blow up the Houses of Parliament. They would do it at the state opening ceremony, when King James I would be present.

The plotters included Robert and Thomas Winter, John and Christopher Wright, Thomas Percy and Guy Fawkes. Fawkes was a Yorkshireman who had fought for the Spanish army in the Netherlands.

The plotters rented a property next to the Houses of Parliament and began digging a tunnel on 11 December 1604. The tunnel became impossible to dig — the foundations of the Houses of Parliament were 9 feet thick.

By luck they found a cellar for rent directly underneath the Houses of Parliament. On 25 March 1605 they stowed 36 barrels of gunpowder there, covered with wood to hide them.

Parliament was not due to be opened until 5 November. As the plotters waited, more wealthy Catholics became part of the plan, including Ambrose Rookwood, Everard Digby and Francis Tresham.

Discovery of the plot

One Catholic lord, Monteagle, did not join the plot but played a crucial part in its discovery. While out on an errand on 26 October 1605, his servant was handed a letter by a tall stranger. The text of this letter is given in Source A.

Lord Monteagle could not make head nor tail of the letter. It was undated, unsigned and badly written. He handed it to the king's chief adviser, Robert Cecil. Cecil took the letter to the king, who at first ignored it. When Cecil asked him to read it again, the king decided that there was to be an attempt to blow up himself and parliament.

There was an immediate search of the cellars of the Houses of Parliament, on 4 November. It discovered only piles of wood, in one cellar.

The king ordered a second search, and this time, at 11 p.m., Guy Fawkes was discovered with the gunpowder, a lantern, a watch and some slow matches. He was arrested and thrown into the Tower of London.

What happened to the plotters?

The rest of the plotters were rounded up on 7 November. They were captured in a gun-fight at Holbeche House in the west Midlands, where they had gone to organise their rebellion. Robert Catesby and Thomas Percy fought back-to-back, and were shot dead with the same bullet.

In the Tower of London, Guy Fawkes signed a confession admitting his part in the plot. He was tried on 27 January 1606 and sentenced to be hung, drawn and quartered.

The terrible execution was carried out on 30 January. Seven other plotters were executed at the same time.

Source A

The Monteagle letter

My lord out of the love i beare to some of youere frends i have a caer of youer preseruacion therfor i would advyse yowe as yowe tender youer lyf to devys some excuse to shift of youer attendance at this parleament for god and man hath concurred to punishe the wickednes of this tyme and think not slightlye of this advertisment but retyre youre self into youre contri wheare yowe may expect the event in safti for thowghe theare be no appearance of anni stir yet i saye they shall receyve a terrible blowe this parleament and yet they shall not seie who hurts them this cowncel is not to be contemned because it may do yowe good and can do yowe no harme for the dangere is passed as soon as yowe have burnt the letter and i hope god will give yowe the grace to mak good use of it to whose holy proteccion i comend yowe.

Activity

1. Look at **Source A**. With a partner, try to write it out in modern English.

2. Read the following statements and place them in chronological order.
   a. The remaining plotters were hung, drawn and quartered.
   b. A plot was hatched to blow up parliament and the king.
   c. Lord Monteagle received an anonymous letter.
   d. A tunnel was started from a room next door to the Houses of Parliament but failed to get through and had to be abandoned.
   e. Thirty-six barrels of gunpowder were brought by barge up the Thames and placed in the cellar.
   f. The leading plotters were killed at Holbeche House.
   g. The plotters rented a cellar directly under the Houses of Parliament.
   h. Fawkes was discovered with the gunpowder and matches at 11 p.m. on 4 November.
   i. The letter was read by the king and he worked out that there was a plot against him.
   j. A search of the cellars found nothing but wood.

3. If you could use only **six** of these statements to help you draw a storyboard of these dramatic events, which six would you choose? Why?

4. Draw your storyboard as if it were going to be made into a drama for television. Remember to include the most dramatic moments.

Topic 2   How hard was it to keep England Protestant?

Facts about the plot

1 The government held a monopoly on the sale of gunpowder.

3 Lord Monteagle had promised the king that he would become Protestant if he was given a place in the House of Lords.

5 Fawkes was tortured on the rack to extract his confession. (The rack stretched all the victim's joints. See the picture on page 10.)

2 The plotters were rounded up at Holbeche House very quickly after the plot had failed.

4 Lord Monteagle was given a life pension by the king after the plot.

18 Most Catholics in England said that they disagreed with the plot and many tried to become more loyal to the English crown. The Pope's influence was beginning to wane.

The plotters

17 Builders excavating the area in 1823 found no trace of a tunnel, or any evidence that a tunnel had been dug.

15 The 36 barrels of gunpowder were handed over to the ordnance depot at the Tower of London. A report there described them as being 'decayed', so the gunpowder was probably useless — it had been left in a damp cellar for 8 months.

14 The gunpowder records for November 1605 went missing shortly after the plot was foiled. They were never found.

16 No one other then Cecil's men saw the barrels of gunpowder.

13 The gunpowder records were kept by the government.

22

6 The Gunpowder Plot was only one of a number of plots against the government at this time.

7 The person who rented out the cellar under the Houses of Parliament was Robert Cecil's best friend. He too was executed, 3 months after the plotters.

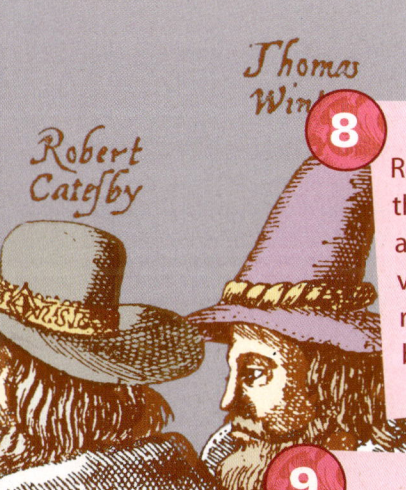

8 Robert Cecil became the king's most trusted adviser, and he became very powerful as a result of the plot being foiled.

9 Cecil had a large number of spies working for him in England.

10 Guy Fawkes's confession was the only evidence that a plot existed.

11 All the plotters were killed, either shot before they could defend themselves, or executed after being tortured to confess.

12 The identity of the author of the Monteagle letter was never discovered.

Activity

1. Read the facts about the plot. They were left out of the 'traditional' story of the plot. Do any facts make you suspicious about the story? Discuss your ideas with a partner.

2. With your partner, choose the **nine** best pieces of evidence to show that the plotters *could not have made the plot*. Decide on their order of importance.

3. Copy the following diagram on to a full page of your exercise book and use it to rank your nine pieces of evidence in order of most important to least important.

Most important ↑

Least important ↓

Overview activity

Write a letter to your MP explaining why Guy Fawkes deserves a pardon. Use the facts about the plot to help make your points. You need to be convincing, so link some of your facts together to show your thinking.

Hint: think about which people benefited from the plot and what their roles were.

Topic 3
Did Charles I throw away the crown of England?

What caused the English Civil War?

The monarchy and Parliament

The monarchy was still a powerful institution. We have seen the power that kings and queens held over the Church. They seemed to be able to change the religion of the country at will.

In 1625, **Charles I**, the son of James I, became King of England. He found himself facing a new challenge to his power, from Parliament.

Parliament had become more powerful. The king had to ask its permission to raise money for particular problems like wars. Usually Parliament agreed to let the king raise taxes. However, it realised that this hold over the king was making it powerful.

Look at the diagram of 'The timeline to war', and think about the issues that divided the king and Parliament.

Charles did not recall Parliament for 11 years.

Charles raised money without the agreement of Parliament.

Charles disbanded Parliament in 1629.

Charles believed that he ruled by divine right (i.e. that his power came straight from God).

In 1625, Charles asked Parliament to raise a tax in order to fight a war with Spain, but it refused.

The king used the Court of Star Chamber (his own court) to fine anyone who spoke against him. The fines were huge.

Charles married Henrietta Maria, a French princess. She was a Catholic.

The king charged people a fee to become a knight. Anyone unwilling to pay was fined heavily.

The king needed the support of Parliament to pass his laws, but he could also dissolve Parliament and rule by himself if he so wished.

In 1634, Charles revived an ancient law on ship money. This was a tax from medieval times, where people living on the coast paid an extra charge to fund ships to defend them against coastal raiders. After 1634 Charles extended the tax inland.

TIMELINE START

Charles I

In 1637, Charles fined William Prynne £5,000 for being a Puritan (an extreme Protestant). His ears were cut off and his cheeks were branded with a hot iron. He was then imprisoned for life. Archbishop Laud felt that the Puritans were becoming too powerful.

The timeline to war

Parliament gave the king a list of grievances in November 1641, demanding changes in the way he ruled. This was called the Grand Remonstrance.

In January 1642, Charles decided that he would show Parliament how powerful he was. He took 300 soldiers to Westminster and tried to arrest five 'troublesome' members of Parliament. The MPs had already escaped in a boat, up the Thames.

On 10 January, Charles left London for Nottingham Castle, where he raised his standard on 22 August 1642. The English Civil War had begun.

TIMELINE END

Parliament accused Archbishop Laud and the Earl of Strafford of treason. In 1641 the king had to allow his two close friends to be executed.

Charles recalled Parliament to ask it for a tax to pay for the war.

In 1640, the Scots invaded northern England. In order to repel them the king needed to raise an army, and to do that he needed money.

Charles recalled Strafford to England in 1639. Would he use troops against his own people?

Charles used troops to force his laws on the Scots and the Irish. The soldiers were led by his trusted friend and adviser, the Earl of Strafford.

Also in 1637, Charles demanded that the Scottish Church use the English prayer book, but it refused, and riots broke out in the churches.

Activity

❶ Which of the alternatives in each pair from the table below do you think was most worrying to the people of England? Make your choices for **a–d** and explain your reasons clearly.

a	The king married a French princess.	OR	The king married a Catholic.
b	The king ruled without Parliament for 11 years.	OR	The king started to raise taxes without Parliament's permission.
c	The king tried to force his changes to the Church on the Scots.	OR	The king tried to arrest members of Parliament.
d	Parliament challenged the king.	OR	The king claimed that his power came from God.

❷ The causes of the Civil War fall into three categories — religion, money and power.

Copy and complete the following table. Read through the points on the timeline to war again and write each one under the relevant heading in your exercise book. The first point has been done for you.

Religion	Money	Power
		The king could dissolve Parliament and rule by himself

Hint: some of the causes might fit into more than one column.

❸ What do you think was the most important reason for the king going to war against his own people?

❹ What do you think was the most important reason for Parliament deciding to challenge the authority of the king?

❺ Is it fair to say that 'England was turned upside down' in the seventeenth century?

Topic 3 Did Charles I throw away the crown of England?

Choosing a side

The two sides

The supporters of Parliament were known as **Parliamentarians**. They were nicknamed '**Roundheads**' because of the severe haircuts that supporters of this side adopted.

The king's supporters were known as **Royalists**. They were nicknamed '**Cavaliers**', an insulting term describing reckless cavalrymen (troops on horseback) from Spain.

For some people the choice was simple — they supported the side that the rest of their family supported. For others the choice was harder.

Who were the supporters?

Look at **Source A**. If you lived in the north of England, how easy would it be to side with Parliament if everyone else was a Royalist? Did a person in a certain area always support the side that everyone else around them supported?

The table in **Source B** shows which groups of people tended to choose each side.

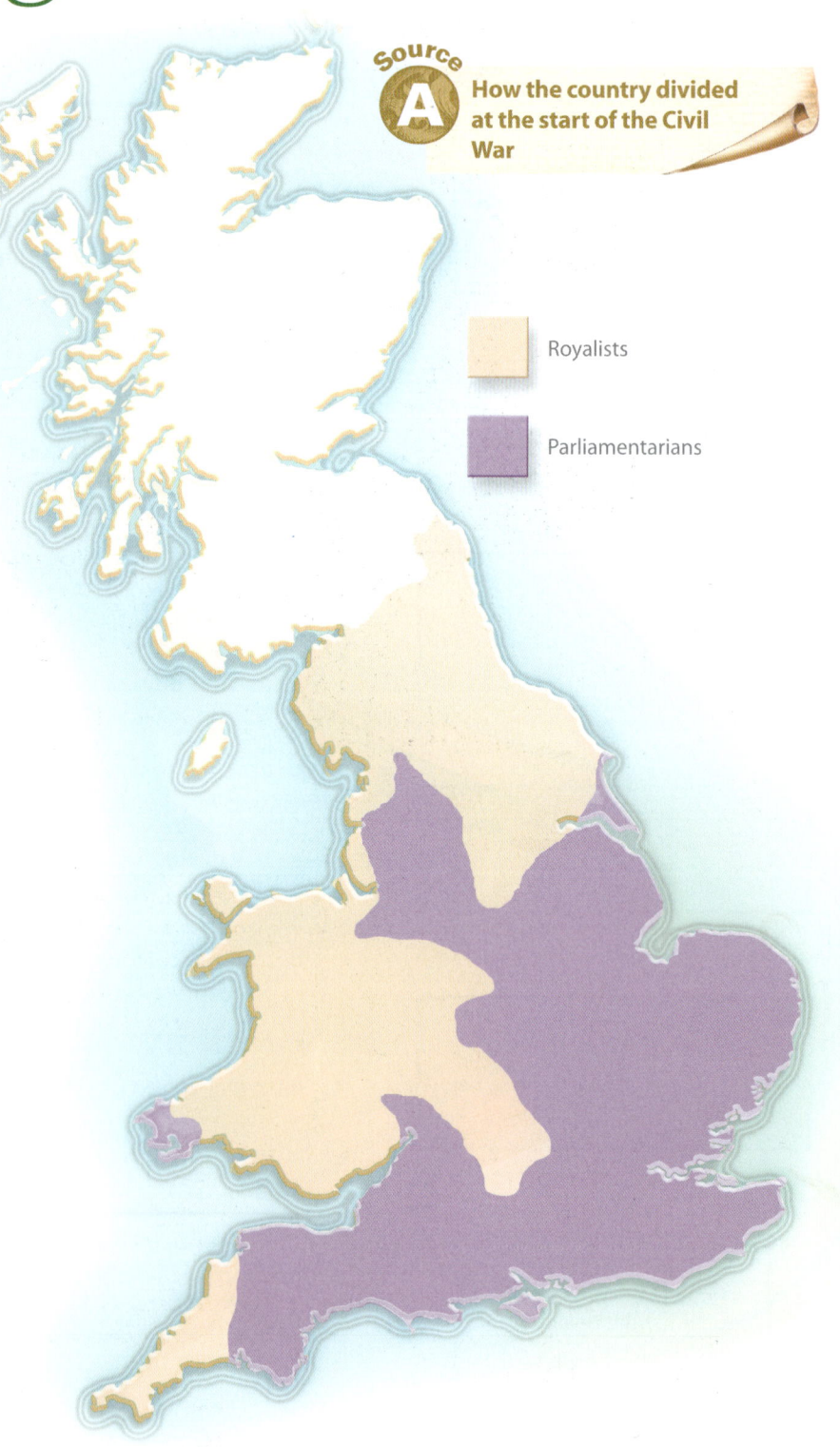

Source A How the country divided at the start of the Civil War

- Royalists
- Parliamentarians

Which side would these people have fought on?

1. I'm a landowner and I'm sick of paying more and more taxes to the king. I don't mind him collecting some taxes, but he's collecting too many.

2. As a lawyer, I think that the laws of the land have to be obeyed. It is wrong to go to war.

3. It isn't right that some businesses are favoured by the monarch.

4. As a Scotsman, I believe that we should be able to do as we please in our own churches.

5. I think that the people we elect should have much more say about what happens in the country.

6. I believe that I am answerable only to God, not to any king.

7. I think that taxes should only be levied (charged) if we, the people who have to pay them, agree.

8. I believe that the Church of England is becoming more Catholic after Laud's changes. It should be even more Protestant, with plainer churches for a start.

9. I believe that the Church of England has been changed for the good of the people. Archbishop Laud was right.

10. I think people should realise that God chooses who should rule. All monarchs should be obeyed.

Source B — Supporters of each side

Royalists	Parliamentarians
Landowning nobles and country gentlemen	Members of Parliament, and the city of London (where Parliament was)
Supporters of the Church of England, especially after the changes introduced by Laud, which allowed for the use of ornamentation in churches and convinced the people that the king was urging a return to Catholicism	People who wanted to make the Church of England more extreme, like the Puritans
Supporters of the Catholic Church	Businessmen and traders, especially in port towns
People in the north and northwest of England	People in the south and southeast of England
People in Wales	Some Irish and Scots
People who lived on the estates of landowning Royalists	People who didn't like the idea of monarchy

Activity

Look at what the people are saying and decide which side they might have supported — Parliament or the king.

Topic 3 Did Charles I throw away the crown of England?

Problems with taking sides

It was not always easy for people to choose one side or the other. Think about the problems that a Catholic might have who lived in London but wanted to support the king. Similarly, a wool merchant in northern England would have difficulty supporting Parliament. (He might want to do this because Parliament opposed the king's right to give monopolies to favoured businessmen.)

In fact, many MPs supported the king, and a number of wealthy northern nobles favoured Parliament. There were no hard and fast rules. Neighbour might end up fighting neighbour.

In one famous example, Sir Edmund Verney, a wealthy landowner, fought on the Royalist side while his son Ralph fought for Parliament. In other instances, brothers found themselves on opposing sides as they could not reconcile their differences (see **Source A**).

Fearful times

People were bound to cover up their true feelings if they thought they would get into trouble for them. As a result, there was a climate of suspicion and fear in England during the Civil War. People looked for clues as to who supported whom.

It was so bad that some would not join either side. Many nobles refused to join in, and did not ask their estate workers to fight either. Some nobles even organised their own private armies to repel soldiers of either side who came near their lands.

When the war began on 22 August 1642, it was almost certain to be long and drawn-out. It did not end until 20 August 1648.

Parliamentarian banner

Activity

1. Which side do you think you would have been on? Write a letter to a friend, explaining who you would have supported and why. What would have influenced you? For instance, which part of the country do you live in? Would that have affected your decision if you'd been alive in 1642? Make sure your letter refers to all the deciding factors as you try to convince your friend that you've made the right choice.

2. Both sides used banners and pennants (small triangular flags) to show who they were and what they believed in. Design a pennant for your chosen side. Think about any symbols that you might use to sum up the ideas your side was fighting for.

Source A

Mystery statements

1. Thomas Burwash (Ralph's brother) had returned from Scotland a devoutly religious person — a Puritan.
2. The New Model Army fought the Cavaliers at Naseby in June 1645.
3. After Naseby, Ralph never saw his parents again.
4. Ralph said he was loyal to the king. He joined Prince Rupert's cavaliers.
5. Charles I believed he ruled by divine right. He was answerable only to God.
6. Thomas said the king and queen were Catholic sympathisers.
7. Ralph saw Roundheads strip clothes and weapons from the dead and dying.
8. From 1629 to 1640 the king ruled without Parliament. This made many people angry.
9. Their mother said Ralph and Thomas were of the same family and would answer to one God.
10. As children, the brothers used to swim after the family helped out with the haymaking.
11. Ralph said the king recalled Parliament to raise money to deal with the Scots.
12. Thomas said Charles recalled Parliament to raise taxes to waste on his family, palaces and paintings.
13. Mary Burwash said she would disown her sons if they fought each other.
14. Ralph thought he saw Thomas fall in a charge on the Royalist cannons.
15. As one of 5,000 prisoners at the Battle of Naseby, Ralph was made to spend the next day digging graves.
16. Thomas joined Cromwell's New Model Army after seeing a recruiting sergeant.
17. Ralph told his mother that Thomas was a 'Scottish rebel'.
18. It is estimated that over 1,000 men died at Naseby from musket, cannon or pike wounds.
19. Thomas had a star-shaped birthmark on his back.
20. Scottish rebels attacked England in 1639.

Overview activity

MYSTERY! Why was Ralph Burwash found drowned in 1646?

The Civil War literally tore families apart as people were forced to take sides according to their convictions. The story of the Burwash brothers tells us something about the difficult decisions that faced many families across the land.

Ralph Burwash was found drowned in 1646, and your job is to suggest why. Use the evidence in statements 1–20 (**Source A**) to support your argument.

1. Read the mystery statements in **Source A**. Your teacher may provide them as separate cards.
2. Sort the statements into four or five categories according to the links you can see between the pieces of evidence.
3. Give a heading of one or two words to each group of statements, e.g. 'Religion' or 'Background'. This will help you to gather your thoughts.
4. Use the evidence to work out what might have happened to Ralph. There is more than one possible answer, and there may be a combination of factors.
5. Justify your story by explaining how the facts support your argument. The more facts you can use, the stronger your answer will be. If you think some facts are less important, say why. Ignore any statements that don't help you explain your story.
6. Write your explanation for why Ralph died in less than 300 words.

Topic 3   Did Charles I throw away the crown of England?

English Civil War battles

English Civil War battles were **pitched battles**, which means that they were set up (a bit like a game of chess). Look at the artist's impression of a Civil War battle. It shows some of the weapons and tactics that were used at the time. You can see where the artillery was placed (the cannon) and the way the different soldiers were positioned at the start of the battle.

❶ Artillerymen
- Huge guns called cannon fired heavy cannon balls to break up the lines of troops.
- Cannon balls didn't explode, but their weight would kill a man.

❷ Buglers
Buglers played above the noise of battle to direct the cavalry.

❸ Cavalrymen
Cavalrymen were the soldiers on horseback who led the charge with swords and pistols. They hurtled towards the enemy to punch a hole through the front line and eventually surround it.

❹ Drummers
The drummers kept advancing foot soldiers in step.

❺ Musketeers
- First, the musket barrel had to be 'charged' (loaded) with gunpowder. Then lead shot (the bullet) was put in, and finally 'wadding' such as cloth was rammed down the barrel.
- Gunpowder had to be put into the 'pan' on the side of the musket. The musketeer took aim with the aid of the musket stand. When the enemy came within range (10 metres), a glowing rope end called a 'match' was used to ignite the main charge and fire the musket.
- The musket was an unreliable weapon, but was cheaper to produce than the more reliable flintlock.

❻ Pikemen
- The pike was a 5-metre long wooden pole with a metal blade on the end.
- Pikemen had to repel the charge of the cavalry. They planted the blunt end of the pike in the ground, under their feet. They then braced themselves for the horses running towards them, and tried to push the pike towards the chest of a horse.
- They also marched towards the enemy with the pike raised at shoulder height in front of them to engage the enemy.

❼ Standard bearers
The flag carriers were a rallying point for the army in the confusion of the battlefield.

Soldiers in action

Battle plan

Pikemen
Musketeers
Cavalry
Artillery

31

Topic 3 Did Charles I throw away the crown of England?

Soldiers in the Civil War had a number of weapons at their disposal, and there were a number of jobs to be done. Armies usually included **cavalrymen** (soldiers on horseback) and **artillerymen** (soldiers who fired cannon). The most common soldiers were the foot soldiers, or **infantrymen**, who were either **pikemen** or **musketeers**.

A Parliamentarian soldier

A Royalist soldier

Activity

1. Copy this Venn diagram into your exercise book.

Parliamentarian — Both — Royalist

Activity

❷ Look at the pictures of the two soldiers. They have several differences and similarities. To help you compare them, find the following items, which could be on either picture or both. Write the letter for each item in the 'Parliamentarian', 'Royalist' or 'Both' section of your Venn diagram.

   a knee-length leather boots
   b leather coat, to give some protection from blows
   c leather gauntlet, to give some protection from blows
   d stirrups, to help rider remain steady in the charge
   e shoulder strap to 'holster' a sword
   f shot or 'bullets' in a round satchel
   g 'lobster-pot' helmet (it looked a bit like a lobster's tail at the back)
   h wide-brimmed hat
   i metal guard on sword to protect the hand in close combat
   j standard carried on the battlefield to show the position of troops to the commanders observing the battle
   k iron breastplate to protect the chest
   l coloured sash to identify which side the soldier was on
   m gunpowder bottle on a belt

❸ Which one of these soldiers do you think was the best protected? Explain your opinion.

❹ What similarities are there between the two soldiers?

❺ How are they different? Can you think of any reasons for these differences?

Look back to the battle picture on pages 30–31. You now have some idea of what a battle looked like. You know what the soldiers had to do and what they wore. Imagine yourself in their position.

❻ Which soldier do you think had the worst job to do? Explain your answer fully.

❼ Which soldier had the most important job? Explain your answer fully.

❽ A battle would be planned thoroughly and would always follow a similar pattern.

   a Look at the following stages of a battle and put them in the correct order:
      ✤ The musketeers advanced behind the pikemen.
      ✤ The artillery opened fire to blast a way through the ranks (lines) of the foot soldiers.
      ✤ The pikemen were commanded to set their pikes in the ground.
      ✤ A parley was held (a meeting in which the time for the battle was set).
      ✤ The musketeers loaded their muskets and fired.
      ✤ The pikemen were ordered to march in a line towards the enemy.
      ✤ The cavalry charged to try to break through the enemy lines.
   b Why would a battle like this not be finished quickly?

❾ Why do you think the English Civil War went on for so long? Think about:
   ✤ which side people supported
   ✤ where they lived
   ✤ how long it might take to raise an army
   ✤ planning a battle
   ✤ training the troops
   ✤ fighting the battle
   ✤ moving on to the next battle

Topic 3 Did Charles I throw away the crown of England?

Where was the English Civil War fought?

The battle of Marston Moor

Phase 1

King Charles I raised his standard at Nottingham Castle on 22 August 1642. This was the beginning of the English Civil War, but the first real battle did not occur until 23 October 1642.

The first battle was at **Edgehill** in Warwickshire. Despite the initial success of the king's cavalry, it was a draw.

The king then felt bolder and made a move for London, but his troops were repelled at **Turnham Green** on 12 November 1642.

It took nearly a year before the armies were ready to fight again. At the battle of **Newbury** in Oxfordshire on 21 September 1643, the king's army again failed to beat that of Parliament.

On 23 November 1643, Parliament joined forces with the Scots. On 2 July 1644 they fought the king's army again, at **Marston Moor** in Yorkshire, and won.

The king was forced into battle again on 14 June 1645,

Battlegrounds

- Preston — 20 August 1648
- Marston Moor — 2 July 1644
- Newark — 5 May 1646
- Naseby — 14 June 1645
- Edgehill — 23 October 1642
- Newbury — 21 September 1643
- Turnham Green — 12 November 1642

Activity

1. What do you notice about the battles and where they were fought?
2. Draw a timeline to show the major battles.
3. A **turning point** is where things change completely. Was there a turning point in the English Civil War?

at **Naseby** in Northamptonshire. This time his army was put to flight. It was a famous victory for the Parliamentarians.

The king did not surrender immediately, but he was putting off the inevitable. He finally stopped running on 5 May 1646, when his army was beaten by the Scots at **Newark** in Nottinghamshire.

Phase 2

It seemed that the war was over, but the king had one more surprise up his sleeve. He made a secret treaty with the Scottish army in May 1648, and the Civil War restarted. This phase did not last as long as the first one. The Scottish army was defeated at **Preston** on 20 August 1648, 6 years, almost to the day, after the war began.

The king had waged war on his people. He had also used foreign troops from Germany and had turned Scotland against Parliament. Here was a man who would be difficult to trust in the future.

Topic 3 — Did Charles I throw away the crown of England?

ICT and numeracy exercise

We have a lot of information about the battles of the English Civil War. You need to decide what is relevant to your investigation. You may also want to arrange data in different ways to see hidden patterns, or to present information in graphic form.

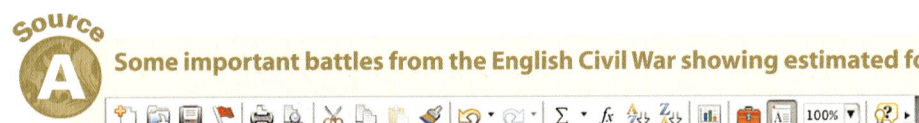

Source A

Some important battles from the English Civil War showing estimated forces and dead

A	B	C	D	E	F	G	H
Battle	Date	County	Victory	Parliamentarian forces	Royalist forces	Parliamentarian dead	Royalist dead
Adwalton Moor	1643-06-30	West Yorkshire	Royalist	4,000	10,000	500	few
Braddock Down	1643-01-19	Cornwall	Royalist	4,000	5,000	200	few
Brentford	1642-11-12	Middlesex	Royalist	4,600	4,600	170	few
Chalgrove	1643-06-18	Oxfordshire	Royalist	1,150	1,000	few	few
Cheriton	1644-03-29	Hampshire	Parliamentarian	10,000	5,000	60	300
Cropredy Bridge	1644-06-29	Oxfordshire	Indecisive	9,000	9,000	700	few
Edgehill	1642-10-23	Warwickshire	Royalist	15,000	15,000	1,000	500
Hopton Heath	1643-03-19	Staffordshire	Indecisive	1,500	1,200	250	250
Langport	1645-07-10	Somerset	Parliamentarian	10,000	7,000	few	few
Lansdown Hill	1643-07-05	Gloucestershire	Indecisive	4,000	6,300	20	300
Marston Moor	1644-07-02	West Yorkshire	Parliamentarian	28,000	18,000	300	4,000
Naseby	1645-06-14	Northamptonshire	Parliamentarian	15,000	12,000	150	1,000
Newbury 1	1643-09-21	Berkshire	Indecisive	15,000	15,000	3,000	3,000
Newbury 2	1644-10-02	Berkshire	Indecisive	19,000	8,500	n/a	n/a
Powick Bridge	1642-09-23	Worcestershire	Royalist	1,000	1,000	40	few
Rowton Heath	1645-09-24	Cheshire	Parliamentarian	4,000	4,000	few	600
Stow on the Wold	1646-03-21	Gloucestershire	Parliamentarian	3,000	3,300	few	200
Stratton	1643-05-16	Cornwall	Royalist	5,600	3,000	300	few
Winceby	1643-10-11	Lincolnshire	Parliamentarian	5,000	3,000	20	300
Worcester	1651-09-03	Worcestershire	Parliamentarian	28,000	12,000	200	3,000

Activity

The spreadsheet in **Source A** shows some of the main battles of the Civil War. They are sorted in alphabetical order of the names of the battles. Data can be sorted using different criteria to make them easier to understand.

1. Enter the data into a new spreadsheet page.

2. Click the top left cell so that the whole spreadsheet is selected.

3. Click on the **Data** option at the top of the page and select Sort from the drop-down menu.

4. A new **Sort** menu will appear and you can sort the data by selecting any of the column names listed (e.g. '**County**'). Remember to select **Header Row** to make sure your heading stays in place.

5. Find answers to the following questions by using the correct columns to sort the information:
   a Were most battles fought in the south of England, the midlands or the north? You may need to refer to an atlas to help you here.
   b Which side won the most battles?
   c Which side won more battles later on in the war?

6. Calculate the total strength and losses for each side by clicking on the empty cell beneath any of the last four columns and then clicking on the **AutoSum** symbol on the toolbar.

   Hint: a data selection box will appear, and you may have to extend it to cover all the cells in your chosen column.

   Then click enter on your keyboard to display the total figure.

7. Once you have calculated the sum of the forces and the losses for each side, you can create a pie chart showing either forces or losses by using the **Chart Wizard**. Remember to select the two sums you wish to represent in the chart.

8. Do you think the data tell us all we need to know about these conflicts?
   a What other information would it be useful to know?
   b Why might these figures not be totally reliable?

Topic 3   Did Charles I throw away the crown of England?

Why did Parliament win?

At the start of the war, the king had several advantages. He had a number of possible allies abroad and his army was better trained. The regular army tended to support the king, while Parliament had more volunteers who came from other walks of life.

In the end, Parliament won the war. There were a number of reasons for this.

The battle of Naseby

Source A

Why did Parliament win the Civil War?

1. There was no such thing as a national army at this time, although the king did have loyal troops.
2. Parliament controlled the richest parts of England, especially the southeast, so it was easier for it to get money.
3. Some nobles were reluctant to give their money to the king.
4. The king's forces found it difficult in many towns to defeat Parliament's army. Townsfolk, especially in London, often joined the Parliamentarians to resist the king — but only while Royalists were threatening the town.
5. The king left London at the start of the war, so it was easier for Parliament to control the main centre of population.
6. Charles did not have the money to pay his soldiers.
7. The king's army often found it difficult to get supplies. The most important example was a shortage of ammunition during 1643.
8. Charles found it increasingly difficult to get help from abroad. The navy controlled the ports and it supported Parliament.
9. Parliament's control of port towns meant that it could get supplies more easily.
10. The king allowed his nephew, Prince Rupert, to command his armies. Rupert, a German prince, was young and inexperienced.
11. Fighting a war for 6 years was expensive. The king did not have access to taxes, but Parliament did. (This was one of the biggest reasons for the war in the first place.)
12. Oliver Cromwell, a Parliamentarian general, trained his soldiers well, so that they became a disciplined fighting force. They were known as the Ironsides.
13. Cromwell's soldiers were guaranteed a wage.
14. A number of Parliament's soldiers were religious men who believed they were doing 'God's will' in fighting the king.
15. Cromwell's soldiers didn't drink to excess.
16. Parliament overhauled the whole of its army, especially its cavalry, to make it like Cromwell's Ironsides. It became known as the New Model Army.
17. Parliament had several able commanders, such as Oliver Cromwell, Thomas Fairfax, Thomas Pryde and George Monck.
18. Prince Rupert made some basic errors in a number of battles. At Naseby he made his cavalry attack too quickly, advancing too far. As a result they were exhausted for the rest of the battle.

Skill box

A **concept map** is a good way of linking all the big issues from the mass of information you already have. Look at the example below, which shows the thinking of one student. The student has begun to make some links between the key factors.

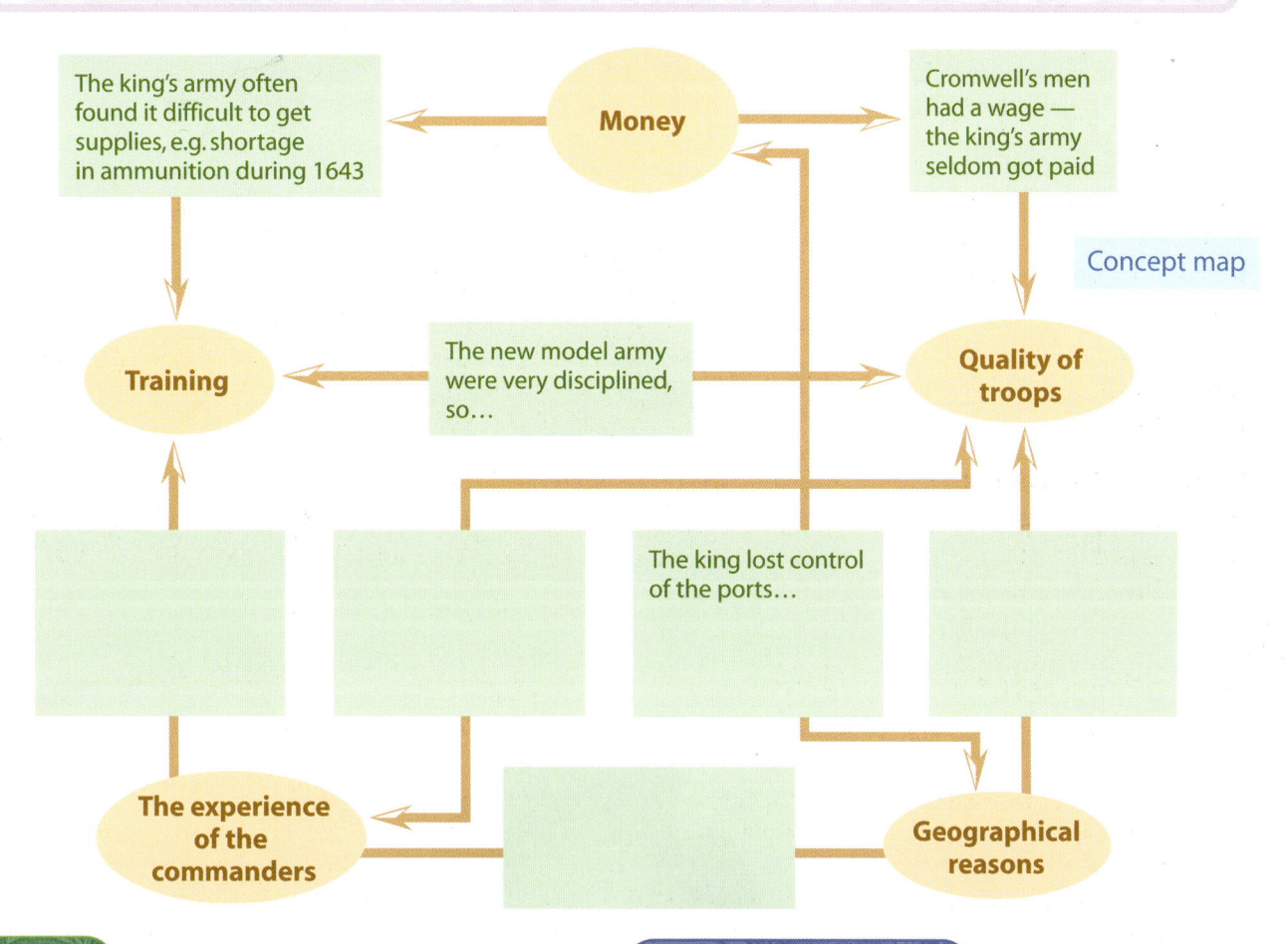

Concept map

- The king's army often found it difficult to get supplies, e.g. shortage in ammunition during 1643
- **Money**
- Cromwell's men had a wage — the king's army seldom got paid
- **Training**
- The new model army were very disciplined, so…
- **Quality of troops**
- The king lost control of the ports…
- **The experience of the commanders**
- **Geographical reasons**

Activity

1. Look at **Source A**. It shows some positive reasons why the Parliamentary forces won the war. It also shows negative reasons why the Royalist forces lost. In your exercise book, make one list of the positive reasons and another of the negative ones.

2. Can you think of any other reasons that should be on the list?

3. Look at the example concept map. Either:
   a. copy this concept map and find evidence to complete it; or
   b. draw your own version by putting your own five key issues on a full page of your exercise book (leave yourself room to write the links)

Overview activity

Use your responses to Activity 1 to answer the essay question:

'Did Charles lose or did Parliament win the Civil War?'

Remember that your essay must have an introduction in which you should give your opinion on the question. Look at your answer to Activity 1 to help you make up your mind. Which column has the most reasons?

The paragraphs that you write after this should all reflect this opinion. If you think Charles lost the war mainly because his generals were poor, the first paragraph after your introduction should explain this and give some examples.

Topic 4
Did kings have to obey the laws of their land?

What should happen to Charles I?

Having won the war, Parliament had one final decision to make. What should be done with the king? Parliament had fought him because he was a tyrant who did not keep to the rules. How should he be dealt with? Look at the options that Parliament had.

Activity

1. If you were a member of Parliament at the time, which of these options would you vote for?
2. Discuss with a partner what the best course of action would be and why the other options are less suitable.
3. Which options might the king disagree with?
4. Read on and see whether your ideas match those of Parliament.

1 Make him promise to be a better king in future by not collecting unfair taxes. Let him continue as king.

2 Make Parliament the only power in the land. This would stop Charles interfering with any aspect of government, including taxes and the religion of the country.

3 Leave the system as it is with Charles I remaining as king. If he continues to rule badly, prevent his son from taking the throne.

4 Invite him to be a member of Parliament as an equal, but still allow him to be called 'the king'.

5 Put him on trial to give him a chance to explain his behaviour and defend himself against the charges.

6 Throw him into jail for the rest of his life.

Charles I

What should be done with the king? Parliament's options

The king on trial

On 20 January 1649, Charles I, the King of England, was put on trial. It had not been an easy decision for Parliament to take, and one that had never been made before. Parliament was not sure how it would work out.

For a start, Parliament had to decide what charges were appropriate for a king. Look at the options that Parliament had.

Activity

5. If you were a member of Parliament at the time, which of these options would you vote for?
6. Discuss with a partner what the best course of action would be and why the other options are less suitable.
7. Which options might the king disagree with?
8. Read on and see whether your ideas match those of Parliament.

Oliver Cromwell

What should the king be charged with? Parliament's options

1. Charge him with theft because of all the money he took unfairly in the form of new taxes (like ship money).

2. Charge him with treason because he seemed to be trying to change the religion of the country.

3. Charge him with treason because he seemed to be trying to change the way the country was run. He wanted to do just as he pleased.

4. Charge him with the murder of all the soldiers from Parliament's side. They were only defending the rights of the people.

5. Charge him for every death, all the destruction and all the problems he caused the people of England in the Civil War.

6. Drop all the charges against him and hope that he would be scared into learning a lesson.

7. Charge him with deception — he lied about surrendering and then restarted the war, with the Scots on his side.

Topic 4   Did kings have to obey the laws of their land?

What was Charles I charged with?

According to **contemporary** accounts, when Charles entered the court, in the House of Commons, he regarded the bench of judges carefully. He was smiling and a little amused by the proceedings. He didn't seem to be taking the trial seriously. Even when the charges were read out to him, he was intent on looking at the MPs to see if there were any friendly faces. Unfortunately for Charles, many of his supporters had stayed away from his trial.

The charges against the king

As you might expect, the charges were very serious indeed. **Source A** shows what Charles was charged with.

Source A — The king's 'crimes'

(He) had a wicked design to create for himself an unlimited power to rule according to his will and to overthrow the rights and liberties of the people. To do this he treacherously waged a war against Parliament and the people. He is thus responsible for all the treasons, murders, rapings, burnings, damage and desolation, caused by the wars. He is therefore a tyrant, traitor and murderer.

tyrant = someone who rules in a ruthless and harsh way

Source B — The scene at the Palace of Westminster, where the trial of the king took place

Activity

1. Look at **Source A**. Which charges might Charles I think were **unfair**? Explain your reasons carefully.

2. Look at the scene in the Palace of Westminster (**Source B**). Can you find the following people and artefacts in the picture?
   a King Charles I
   b John Bradshaw, the President of the Court
   c armed guards with pikes
   d the **sceptre** that shows the power of the court
   e members of the public there to witness the trial
   f the Recorder, the person who writes down what is said in court

3. Are there any people in the picture who look as though they may be a jury?

4. Looking at the picture as a whole, what clues are there that this was a very important event?

The king's answer

Faced with these serious charges, the king had to defend himself in the court. The king was faced with some hostile MPs who wanted him to explain and justify his actions. It must have been a very difficult atmosphere for the king to speak in, let alone defend himself. Look at the options that the king had.

How should the king defend himself? Charles I's options

Charles I

1 Plead guilty to the charges and hope that this admission might make the court treat him less harshly.

2 Remain silent and not answer the charges in any way.

3 Tell Parliament that as King of England he rules by **divine right**: only he can make the laws, and the court is therefore illegal.

4 Plead guilty and tell the court that he was only defending the rights of the people.

5 Say it should be Parliament that stands trial for treason for having opposed its king.

6 Delay the trial for as long as possible and hope that a foreign power might send troops to free him.

7 Offer to **abdicate** (step down from the throne) in favour of his young son, Charles.

Activity

5. If you were an adviser to the king at the time, which of these options would you suggest?

6. Discuss with a partner what the best course of action would be and why the other options are less suitable.

7. Which options might the king disagree with?

8. Read on and see whether your ideas match those of the king.

Topic 4 — Did kings have to obey the laws of their land?

How should Charles I be punished?

Charles's defence

One hundred and thirty-five High-Court justices were invited to try the king. They were to act as both judge and jury to decide the king's guilt or innocence. Only 68 attended the trial.

Charles I decided to challenge the court's authority to try him. He even refused to remove his hat while in court. He told the court that he was the rightful king, who ruled by divine right, so he could not be put on trial.

The court's response

This was not the best defence to choose. Charles was removed from the court and the trial went on. The king was found guilty of the charges described in **Source A** on page 42.

How should the king be punished? This was the most important decision the court had to take. Look at the options that the Parliamentary court had.

1. Ask the king to abdicate, and put his son Charles on the throne.

2. Send the king away in exile to a foreign country like France, where his wife came from.

3. Put the king in prison, as he is guilty of crimes like theft.

4. Sentence the king to death, as he is guilty of treason.

5. Abolish the role of king and make Charles Stuart an ordinary citizen like everyone else.

6. Fine him for all the damage he did to the country and make him pay compensation, but still allow him to be king and rule alone.

7. Make him accept that Parliament is the only power in England and require him to agree to all Parliament's rules from now on.

Oliver Cromwell

How should the king be punished? Parliament's options

Activity

1. If you were an adviser to Parliament at the time, which of these options would you vote for?
2. Explain to your partner what the best course of action would be and why the other options are less suitable.
3. Which options might the king not accept?
4. Read on and see whether your ideas match those of Parliament.

The sentence

Parliament decided to sentence the king to death, but it was not an easy decision. Only 40 of the judges signed the king's death warrant willingly. A further 12 were coerced into signing it. The rest refused.

This was a momentous decision to take, and things could never be the same again. The death warrant, signed by the 52 judges, remains in the National Records Office to this day.

Why was the execution of the king such a difficult decision for Parliament? Why were people so worried about it? The question of whether Charles I had been treated fairly was also at the forefront of people's minds. People were worried about what the future might hold.

Activity

5 It is 27 January 1649. You are one of the judges who signed the death warrant. Write a speech to persuade the rest of Parliament that they are doing the right thing in executing the king. As you write it, think about:
- the king's 'crimes'
- the king's attitude to the court
- the other choices that Parliament had in dealing with the king
- what you intend to do about ruling the country

If you are going to be successful in persuading people that you are right, you will have to do two things well:
- Find evidence of the worst things that the king did and show how all the other punishments would not have worked.
- Think about the sorts of words you can use to make people see your view. For example, will you call Charles a 'bad ruler', or will you refer to him as a 'tyrant'? One of these options makes him sound much worse than the other. You can make your argument more persuasive by choosing suitable **adjectives** (words that describe people and their actions).

Best of luck in your speech writing. If you aren't successful in persuading people, maybe they will want to get rid of your government next!

The death warrant for Charles I

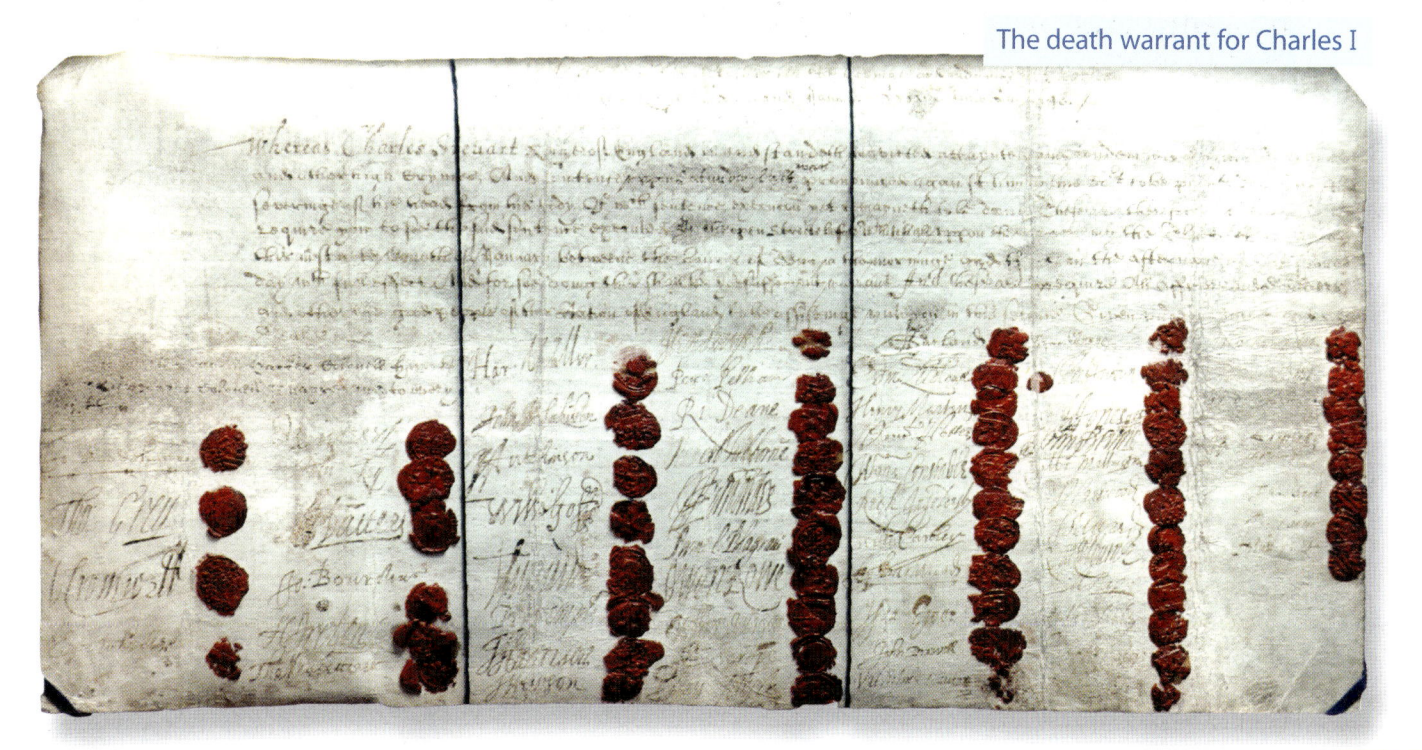

Topic 4   Did kings have to obey the laws of their land?

How popular was the execution of Charles I?

Source A: A contemporary painting of the execution of Charles I

The king's execution was set for Tuesday 30 January 1649. It was a cold and gloomy day. It was frosty and there was snow on the ground as Charles was brought by horse and cart to one of his own palaces, Whitehall.

Preparations

The scaffold was already prepared in front of the palace and the crowd had been gathering from an early hour. It had proved difficult to find an executioner who was prepared to do the job.

Source B: A contemporary engraving of the execution of Charles I

Several executioners refused, even though the fee offered was £100 — a huge amount of money in 1649. Eventually, two men agreed to carry out the execution on one condition. They would do it if they could wear masks and wigs to hide their identities from the king. Some said it was to hide from the glare of God.

Activity

1. Look at **Sources A** and **B**; they show the same event, but Source B was made first. What evidence is there that these are pictures of the same event?
   a. Make a list of points that are the same in each picture and another of the differences.
   b. Which picture do you think:
      - gives the most reliable account of the execution, and why?
      - was intended to be sympathetic towards the king?
2. How does **Source D**:
   a. agree with what you can see in **Sources A** and **B**?
   b. add more information than the pictures convey?
   c. show that historians need a wide range of sources to understand historical events?

The king's arrival

Soldiers crowded round the scaffold, which was draped in black cloth. They were there to prevent the crowd from rescuing the king.

At nearly two o'clock Charles stepped through a window out of the palace and onto the scaffold. He made a speech to the waiting crowd (**Source C**). In the open air of Whitehall, few people would have heard his words.

Source C: The king's final speech from the scaffold

…A subject and a sovereign are clear different things.…If I would have given way…I need not have come here.…All the world knows that I did not begin a war with the two Houses of Parliament. As to the guilt of these enormous crimes that are laid against me, I hope in God that God will clear me of it; I will not. God forbid that I should lay it upon the two Houses of Parliament. I do hope that they are free of this guilt. I am the martyr of the people.

Adapted from 'Aylett, J. *In Search of History* and Adams, R. and Waugh, S. *Think History 1500-1750*

The execution

After his speech, the king removed his outer clothing and his jewels. He had asked his servant to lay out an extra shirt because of the bitter cold. He didn't want people to think that he was shaking with fear if he shivered. He laid his head on the block and prayed. After he had made an agreed signal to the executioner, the axe fell. His head was severed in one blow. This was a rare feat in executions. An eyewitness described the scene (**Source D**).

Source D: An eyewitness account of the execution

I stood amongst the crowd in the street and saw what was done, but was not near enough to hear anything that was said. I saw the blow given with a sad heart… there was such a groan by the thousands then present, as I have never heard before and desire I may never hear again…a troop came marching…to disperse and scatter the crowd, so that I had much trouble in escaping home without much hurt.

The reaction of the crowd

The executioner held the severed head aloft to the crowd, saying: 'Behold the head of a traitor.' The crowd rushed forward and people dipped their handkerchiefs in the king's blood. Some plucked hair from his head and beard. As they did so, troops struggled to disperse the crowd.

Days later the king's head was sewn back on to the body. The corpse was secretly taken to Windsor Castle to be buried.

Overview activity

Write a paragraph to support or contradict the following statement:
'The execution of Charles I was the end of the monarchy for the people of England.'

Topic 5
Was Cromwell really just another king?

Who should rule England instead of the king?

Starter activity

Look at **Source A**. What evidence is there that this is a picture of a king of England? What style of picture is it? What can you guess about the artist's intentions in producing this picture?

Source A — Oliver Cromwell: successful general in the New Model Army. The next King of England?

After the execution of King Charles I, England faced an uncertain future. Who should rule now that the king had gone? Who could rule? There was no doubt that the next person could not be another king.

Parliament would have to rule alone. When a country is ruled without a monarch it is called a **republic**.

This was not the only idea about how the country should be ruled. A number of groups had contrasting ideas about what should happen to England. Some of them are given in **Sources B–F**.

There were still many people who believed that whatever system they adopted, they would be punished by God for what they had done to the king. They thought that this new England was doomed.

48

Source B: The Levellers

A group of Puritans (extreme Protestants) who believed:
- All men are equal.
- All men should vote in elections for Parliament.
- The death penalty should be abolished except for the crime of murder.
- All men should be free to follow any religion they choose.
- Some female Levellers wanted equal rights for women too. This was an astounding idea in the seventeenth century.

Source C: The Diggers

A group who believed:
- All men and women are equal.
- All land should be shared out and farmed in communes.
- All people should share their possessions.

Source D: The Quakers

A group of Puritans who believed:
- All men and women are equal.
- All men and women are entitled to speak in church meetings.
- There is no need to have organised services led by ministers.
- They should welcome anyone into their meeting houses.
- They should love all mankind.
- No one is better than anyone else in society, so nobody deserves more respect than others.
- No cause is worth the use of violence.

Source E: The Fifth Monarchists

A group of poorer people, including some Parliamentarian soldiers, who believed:
- All men are equal. Fifth Monarchists refused to acknowledge anyone else's higher status.
- The return of Jesus Christ to Earth was imminent.
- Earth had to be cleansed so that Jesus could return and rule (this was known as the **Fifth Monarchy**).
- There would have to be a revolt to bring about this change.
- All members of Parliament should be God-fearing people.
- There should not be elections.

Source F: The Ranters

A group who believed:
- All men are equal.
- All men and women should behave in any way they wanted, as Jesus Christ had died for their sins.
- Smoking, drinking, swearing and adultery are acceptable.
- Some Ranters had magical powers and could raise the dead from their graves.

Activity

Although Parliament ruled England after the execution of Charles I, different groups had specific interests they wished to promote.

1. Look at **Sources B–F**.
   a. Make a list of the ideas and beliefs that all the groups agreed on.
   b. Which of these beliefs do you think were realistic ambitions?
2. Which groups focused on religious views, and which focused on political views?
3. If you were a member of Parliament, could you come up with a way of ruling the country that would satisfy all the groups?
4. If you were a member of Parliament, which group would you be most concerned about? Explain your view carefully.

Topic 5 Was Cromwell really just another king?

How 'king-like' was Oliver Cromwell?

Cromwell dissolving the Rump Parliament

Parliament in 1649

Despite all the different groups, the **Long Parliament**, as it was called, had maintained control. However, there had been a number of changes since it began to sit in 1640. For one thing, the king's supporters had left Parliament. There were now only 50 MPs who attended regularly.

It became known as the **Rump Parliament**. This was hardly the government that people had fought a civil war for.

Oliver Cromwell

Cromwell was a farmer from Cambridgeshire. He had been a Puritan MP before the war and emerged as a strong commander during the war.

His retraining of the New Model Army was a decisive factor in Parliament's victory.

Cromwell's views were important to many people. He hoped that the Rump Parliament would allow greater freedom for people, especially in their choice of religion. This was not the case.

50

Cromwell's dilemma

Cromwell was faced with a difficult choice. He could intervene and demand fresh elections that would take account of the new opinions you have been reading about. Or he could take charge himself and ensure the changes took place.

He asked Parliament to hold new elections, but it refused. As taxes began to rise, Cromwell decided that enough was enough. He took a detachment of troops to Parliament in April 1653 and drove out the MPs.

The Barebones Parliament

Cromwell decided that instead of having an election for Parliament, he would choose a Parliament of worthy people to run the country. He asked Puritans around the country to recommend people. He then selected 140 individuals, who he referred to as 'saints', to sit in Parliament.

This was known as the **Barebones Parliament**. It lasted from July until December 1653, but its achievements were small. The parliament agreed on one thing — it abolished itself.

Activity

❸ It is time to add a second arrow to your 'kingometer'. Did Cromwell behave more like a king or a Parliamentarian in the episode of the Barebones Parliament July–December 1653? Remember to give a reason for your arrow.

Cromwell as Lord Protector

After this setback, a group of army officers acting for Parliament asked Cromwell to become the **Lord Protector of England**. They insisted he should work with a Council chosen by Parliament, so they could keep a check on his power.

Cromwell found he could not rule effectively, so he dismissed the parliament in September 1654. Two years later, he did the same again. Was he behaving like a king?

Activity

In 1653, Cromwell could either behave like a king and use his army to enforce his will, or he could trust Parliament and hold elections. As each event unfolds, you are going to decide whether Cromwell was becoming more like a king or more like a Parliamentarian. The 'kingometer' below is a quick way for you to show this.

More like a king

More like a Parliamentarian

❶ Copy the diagram into your exercise book.
❷ Decide whether Cromwell behaved more like a king or a Parliamentarian in April 1653. Draw an arrow on the diagram to show your decision. Write an explanation on your arrow to say why you have placed it where you have.

Hint: did the king ever arrive at Parliament with soldiers?

Activity

❹ Add a third arrow to your 'kingometer'. Did Cromwell behave more like a king or a Parliamentarian as Lord Protector in September 1653? Remember to give a reason for your arrow.

Topic 5 — Was Cromwell really just another king?

The Major Generals

Cromwell adopted a new idea. In August 1655 he divided the country into 11 military districts. Each district was to be run by a force of soldiers under the command of a 'Major General'.

The gentry in each district were charged a tax to maintain the soldiers. Many people saw this as a tax on Royalists, a spiteful revenge for the Civil War. The generals were ruthless in their control.

Even this attempt to control the country did not work. The people hated the strict control of the generals and they began to see Cromwell in the same light. Cromwell dismissed the generals in 1657.

King Oliver?

There seemed to be few options left open to Parliament and Cromwell. Some people in Parliament thought that only a monarchy could save the country from anarchy.

Parliament offered Cromwell the crown of England in 1657. Anyone, it seemed, was better than Charles I's son, Charles Stuart. Cromwell refused. He was afraid the army might not support him.

However, Cromwell arranged for his son, Richard, to succeed him as Lord Protector.

Activity

1. Read the section on 'The Major Generals' and add a fourth arrow to your 'kingometer'. Did Cromwell behave more like a king or a Parliamentarian in this episode? Remember to give a reason for your arrow.
2. Finally, do the same with the section on 'King Oliver?' (And don't forget to add the reason for your fifth arrow!)

Portrait of Oliver Cromwell

Back to monarchy

On 3 September 1658, Oliver Cromwell died of pneumonia. His son became the new Lord Protector, but this still did not bring any stability to the system. Richard Cromwell did not really want the job and the army eventually forced him to stand down in May 1659.

With no other option, the army and Parliament decided that England needed a monarchy. Eleven years after the great experiment began, the former king's son, **Charles II**, returned to the throne.

This return was called the **Restoration**. A king was restored to the throne, ending a period that historians have called the **Interregnum**.

Signs of Charles II's kingship

Activity

3 'Interregnum' is a Latin word meaning a 'period without a king'. Look at your 'kingometer'. Do you agree that this was a period without a king? Explain your answer carefully.

4 Look at the portrait of Oliver Cromwell opposite.
  a How does this portrait show Cromwell as a strong leader?
  b Is there any evidence in this picture that Cromwell wanted to be remembered as a king?
  c Which caption would be the best to place under this portrait: 'Oliver Cromwell — the man responsible for bringing the rule of the generals', or 'Oliver Cromwell — the man who tried to do the right thing for his country'? Explain your choice.

Overview activity

1 Look back at the caricature of Cromwell as a king on page 48. Draw your own caricature of Cromwell, showing what he did when he was in charge. Try to show the good things that he tried to do. For example, he did not accept the title of 'King' and he tried to work with Parliament.

2 Read through the following statements. If they are true, write them down in your exercise book. If they are false, change them to make them true:
  a Oliver Cromwell was always determined to rule as a king.
  b Parliament never had a chance to rule by itself.
  c The army was important in determining who ruled.
  d Cromwell behaved like a king by making his son his successor.
  e Cromwell forced people to obey his rules.
  f Cromwell never shared his power with anyone.
  g Cromwell was more like a military dictator, who used the army to scare people into doing what he wanted.
  h The Royalists would be happy after the Restoration, as Charles I's son became king.
  i The Interregnum followed the Restoration.
  j The Interregnum was an experiment in how England should be ruled.

Topic 5   Was Cromwell really just another king?

What was it like to live under Cromwell's rule?

As you have seen, between 1653 and 1658 Oliver Cromwell was responsible for running the country. It was not a completely happy period for the people of England.

Cromwell, the man who desposed the king, made himself Lord Protector with a salary of £100,000 per year. England was ruled by the army after 1655. Major Generals loyal to Cromwell ensured that new laws were enforced.

Windows like this were smashed

Source A

Changes and new rules

1. Puritans dominated the government. They were extreme Protestants who wanted to purify the Church.
2. Puritans wore simple clothes that were coloured black, grey or white.
3. Puritans insisted that theatres were closed.
4. Puritans banned football, and people were whipped if they played on Sundays (even children).
5. Soldiers confiscated meat from people's tables on Christmas Day.
6. People who swore were fined heavily.
7. People who worked on Sunday were sent for a night in the stocks.
8. Cromwell liked to drink and feast, and he went hunting and enjoyed music.
9. All stained-glass windows were smashed and replaced with plain glass.
10. Statues were removed from the churches.
11. Organs were removed from the churches.
12. Puritans insisted that inns were closed.
13. Puritans insisted that cock-fighting and bear-baiting were abolished.
14. Puritans introduced a fasting day every month.
15. Puritans banned feasting on religious days. They even banned mince pies.
16. Puritans banned the use of holly and other Christmas decorations.
17. People who continued to swear were sent to prison.
18. People who went out for a walk on Sunday were fined.

Activity

❶ New laws were passed by Cromwell during the period. In **Source A** you can see some of the things that happened as a result. As you read them, decide which ones were likely to upset people most.

❷ Make a large copy of the target (right). Choose ten rules from **Source A** that you think people at that time would have been angry about, and place them on your target. Put the ones that people would have **hated most** nearest to the centre.

❸ Look back at the different groups who were hoping for a change in the way England was governed (page 49). Think about whether they would have liked any of the rules from **Source A** or not. Copy and complete the following table.

Group	Rules that might help them get what they wanted
Levellers	
Diggers	
Quakers	
Fifth Monarchists	
Ranters	

❹ Use the target and the table to answer the following question: Do you think Cromwell was a popular ruler or not? Give at least **three** reasons to support your opinion.

Another point of view

When you read the new rules in Source A you should remember Cromwell's title of Lord Protector. He was trying to protect the people of England and to offer them a chance of a more 'godly' life.

It is also worth remembering that England had just survived the Civil War and had faced rebellions from the Scots and the Irish. Firm control was necessary.

To help people become more tolerant, Cromwell stopped newspapers printing whatever they wanted. For some people this looked like press censorship, but Cromwell's motivation was more positive than it first appears.

Activity

❺ When you have read 'Another point of view', look at Source A again and think why the rules might have been made. This time, try to find at least three that you can see positive reasons for. For example, the theatres were closed so that people would concentrate on their religion without any distractions. For some people this was a good step, as the theatre was often rude and much more risqué than today.

Topic 5   Was Cromwell really just another king?

How should we remember Cromwell?

When Oliver Cromwell died, he was given a huge and respectful funeral. Two years later, when Charles Stuart was restored to the throne as Charles II, Cromwell's body was dug up and taken to Tyburn, where common criminals were executed, and it was hung. His head was severed from his body and put on a stake.

Source A is a **memorial** to Cromwell. Why would anyone put his statue outside the entrance to Parliament in Westminster?

You are going to design a new memorial to Cromwell. To be able to do this fairly, you need to know more about his 'reign'.

Cromwell as a general

When the Civil War ended in 1649, Cromwell took the New Model Army to Ireland to quell the rebellion that had begun in 1641. When the troops reached Drogheda, they were determined to exact revenge for the killing of Protestants by the Irish Catholics.

In the stronghold of Drogheda, called Mill Mount, Cromwell's troops slaughtered 2,000 men. Cromwell admitted this in a letter to the House of Commons. Even when some men surrendered the following day, Cromwell ordered that every tenth man be killed as a lesson to the rest.

Churches were burned, some with people in them. There were many gruesome stories. In one story, a Catholic baby was nailed to the church doors as a lesson to Irish Catholics.

Cromwell as Protector

Immediately after the Civil War, there were various groups with different views on how England should be governed (see page 49). One group, the Levellers, rose up to challenge the government.

The 1,000 rebels were cornered by Cromwell's troops in Burford in Oxfordshire. Many of them gave up as soon as they saw the 2,000 troops, but over 300 of them were prepared to fight. They took refuge in Burford church for 3 days before they surrendered. Cromwell had three of the rebels shot in front of the rest as an example to them.

Cromwell as defender of Parliament

When the New Model Army returned from Ireland, it had to quell rebels in Scotland. These were led by Charles I's son, who was calling himself Charles II.

The Scots were defeated in battles at Dunbar in 1650 and Worcester in 1651. Charles fled to France, but he returned to be king in 1660.

Cromwell as leader

You have already seen some of Cromwell's laws (see page 54). Many of them seemed harsh and restrictive. He also kept control by using his soldiers, especially during the rule of the Major Generals from 1655 to 1657.

However, Cromwell did make some positive changes. He believed the whole of the country should share in its wealth, and he called it the **Commonwealth**. There were a number of taxes on the richer people, so poor people paid less.

Fewer crimes were punished by executions. More people were

Source A

Cromwell's statue outside Westminster

Activity

Look at **Source A**. This memorial doesn't give the whole story of Cromwell's life and achievements. Decide what you think this memorial represents, and then design a new memorial to Cromwell showing a different aspect of his life.

Annotate your design with labels to explain what you are trying to show.

---

allowed to worship freely in private. Cromwell also allowed Jews to live and worship in England. They had been banned since the thirteenth century.

More importantly, he built a strong navy to protect the country from foreign invasion. The navy claimed Jamaica for England in 1655. It was the start of England's empire.

Cromwell as a man

Cromwell was not a vain man. For his portrait, instead of the usual flattering picture, he asked to be painted 'warts and all'. He enjoyed music and good food, and valued people's honesty above all other things.

His reputation was fierce. Well into the nineteenth century, parents told their children that if they didn't behave, 'Old Oliver will have you'. In some people's eyes, he was a bogeyman.

Overview activity

An **obituary** is an account of a person's life that appears after their death. It looks at all aspects of their life to give a balanced judgement on their achievements. Write one for Cromwell, in no more than 75 words.

Topic 6
How powerful were kings and queens?

What happened to the power to rule?

The restoration of the monarchy seemed to some people like a betrayal of all that had been won in the Civil War. Most people, however, thought it ended an experiment in government that had gone very wrong. One thing was certain — future monarchs could not rule the way Charles I had done… or could they?

Charles II (1660–85)

Charles was similar to his father in that he did not want to rule with Parliament. He **revoked** (took back) all the laws passed between 1641 and 1660 and started again. He punished all Cromwell's allies and helpers.

Charles reinstated the Church of England, although he was secretly a Catholic. There was violence in London after Titus Oates claimed that some Catholics were planning to massacre Protestants in the city. This became known as the **Popish Plot**. It was only a rumour, yet it was typical of the suspicion that surrounded the monarchy and religion.

Portrait of Charles II

Charles took many mistresses — the most famous was the actress Nell Gwyn. This made him unpopular with the Puritans, as did his revival of the theatres and the arts. His nickname was the 'Merry Monarch'.

He also clashed with Parliament when it asked him to guarantee that his Catholic brother, James, would never become king. Charles spent the last 4 years of his reign ruling without Parliament, just as his father had done. On his deathbed he admitted to being a Catholic.

Activity

1. Make a monarchy trading card for Charles II. Use the example showing what a card for his father might look like to help you.

A monarchy trading card for Charles I

Charles Stuart/Charles I

Reign: 1625–49
Religion: Protestant
Biggest achievement: found lots of ways to raise money without having to beg Parliament.
Biggest mistake: declared war on Parliament and lost.
Relationship with Parliament (rating out of 10): 0 — failed to govern with Parliament and ended up fighting it.
Overall monarchy rating (out of 10): 2 — ended up upsetting many people and didn't curb his spending.

James II (1685–88)

James was a Roman Catholic, like his brother Charles, and made no secret of the fact. He encouraged Catholics to worship freely. This was exactly what Parliament had feared.

Events took a sinister turn when James started to expand his army and place Catholics in command of it. Any rebellions against him, like the Monmouth rebellion in 1685, were dealt with ruthlessly. The rebels were executed or sold into slavery.

James appointed Catholic ministers in the government to replace those who opposed him. He put bishops on trial if they disagreed with him. He dismissed Parliament if it did not do as he wished.

James's heirs

James's wife bore him two daughters, Mary and Anne, both of whom were Protestants. After his first wife's death, James married a Catholic, Mary of Modena. She miscarried several children, but in 1687, at the age of 50, James had a son. He would be raised as a Catholic. Parliament was horrified at the thought of another Catholic king.

There were doubts about whether the baby boy was really the king and queen's. Rumours began that he had been smuggled into the queen's bedchamber in a warming pan (a device containing hot coals, used to warm the bed).

James is deposed

Parliament decided to act. It invited James's daughter Mary and her husband, the Protestant William of Orange, to come to rule instead of James. They accepted, and in 1688 they landed in England. James's army deserted and he fled to France. The story goes that he threw the crown jewels into the River Thames.

Parliament called this the **Glorious Revolution**, because it had changed the monarch without starting another civil war.

Portrait of James II

Activity

❷ Make a monarchy trading card for James II.

James II

Reign:
Religion:
Biggest achievement:
Biggest mistake:
Relationship with Parliament (rating out of 10):
Overall monarchy rating (out of 10):

William and Mary (1688–1702)

William of Orange was a Dutch Protestant prince. He was asked to rule because he was married to the daughter of Charles II. They ruled together.

They accepted some new laws from Parliament, such as the **Bill of Rights** in 1689. This stated that Parliament alone could decide on taxes. It also stated that Parliament was to make the laws, that there could be no army unless it was under Parliament's control and that the monarch had to be Protestant. William and Mary agreed to these conditions.

Topic 6 How powerful were kings and queens?

William and Mary

The **Triennial Act** of 1694 ensured that there were elections to Parliament every 3 years. It was certain that from this point forwards, Parliament was in charge.

The triumph of Protestantism

In 1690, James II tried to reclaim his throne with the help of a Catholic Irish army. Parliament granted William funds to take his army across the Irish Sea to fight James. He defeated James and the Irish at the Battle of the Boyne. It was James's final attempt to regain his crown. William's popularity soared.

Mary died in 1694, childless. Her sister, Anne, was named as her successor, as the **Act of Settlement** (passed in 1701) stated that only a Protestant could rule England and there were no close alternatives. William died in 1702.

Anne (1702–14)

Anne was the last surviving Stuart monarch, the youngest daughter of James II. She resisted all her father's attempts to persuade her to follow Catholicism. She also resisted the temptation to meddle with Parliament. She never dismissed it; in fact she relied on it to rule for her.

Anne had several trusted advisers and appointed a favourite, Marlborough, as her Commander in Chief of the army. She made him a duke and gave him land as a reward for his heroic victory over the French at the Battle of Blenheim in 1704.

In 1707, Parliament passed the **Act of Union** with Scotland. Parliament now ruled Scotland as well as England and Wales. The three countries together were known as the **United Kingdom**. The Scots were not entirely happy and this was to cause problems in the future.

Despite 18 pregnancies, Anne never had a child who lived long enough to be an heir. When she died there was a crisis because there was no one to succeed her.

George I (1714–27)

The nearest in line was George, a German prince from Hanover. He spoke little English and was not particularly interested in ruling England. His first advisers were German and most of his business was conducted in French.

In the first year of his reign, George stopped the Jacobite rebellion (Jacobites were supporters of James Stuart, James II's son).

George I

George then enlisted a politician named Robert Walpole as his prime adviser. The title of 'prime minister' has stuck to this day. In 1716, parliaments were allowed to sit for 7 years before elections had to be held.

Peace and prosperity

George set about making alliances with other countries, such as France and the Netherlands in 1717, and Prussia in 1725. Trade began to grow. Despite scandals such as the South Sea Bubble in 1720, when people who bought shares lost large amounts of money, the United Kingdom became prosperous. At the time of his death, there was peace.

George II (1727–60)

George carried on the work of his father, George I. He even gave Robert Walpole an official residence in 10 Downing Street. He continued to make allies abroad and secured the island of Gibraltar. This increased Britain's naval power in the Mediterranean Sea. He gave small religious groups like the Methodists the freedom to worship; but he also introduced censorship of plays in 1737. The words for 'God save the king' (the National Anthem) were introduced in 1744.

George involved Britain in a war fighting for Austria in 1740. There was also the continuing problem of the Jacobite rebels in Scotland, who rose up again in 1745. The grandson of James II, 'Bonnie Prince Charlie', and his supporters were defeated brutally at the Battle of Culloden, and the threat of rebellion passed.

Britain's wealth and power began to grow with trade routes to the East Indies. A colony in Halifax, Nova Scotia, was founded in 1749. When George died in 1760 Britain was on the verge of even greater prosperity as the Industrial Revolution began to take effect.

Activity

Make monarchy trading cards for William and Mary, Anne, George I and George II.

George II

Overview activity

Compare all your monarchy trading cards to help you answer the following questions:
a Which monarch **lost** the most power?
b Which monarch **gave up** the most power?
c Which monarch was the last who could claim to be in real control of the country?
d What happened to the power of the monarchy between the reigns of Charles I and George II? Make a list of the changes.
e Do you think that Britain was indeed a 'United Kingdom' by 1760? Explain your answer carefully.
f Who was the best monarch during this period?

Topic 7
Was England cursed by evil?

'Evil' in seventeenth-century England

Source A What do you think is happening in this picture?

Starter activity

Look at **Source A**, an engraving made in the seventeenth century. Can you work out what is going on? Who are the three men in black? What are the two men doing with the rope? Who is in the boat in the millpond?

Many people think that the picture in **Source A** shows a punishment for a crime. For people in the seventeenth century, it was more serious than that. It shows an **ordeal**.

The ordeal was a way for judges to find out whether someone was innocent or guilty. People believed that it let God decide the person's innocence or guilt. This cold-water ordeal was used for the crime of **witchcraft** (see clue 13 on page 65).

In the period 1500–1750, it was common for people to be accused of witchcraft. However,

62

until the 1650s it was not common for people to be executed for being a witch.

Who were witches?

It was easy to discover witches, as they had the mark of the devil. People believed that every time the devil bought a soul, he would mark the person's body. The mark could be a birthmark or a mole, or anything out of the ordinary.

To test it, the mark would be struck with a sharp point known as a **bodkin** to make it bleed. If it didn't bleed, or the person felt no pain, it was the mark of the devil. People also believed that the mark was used by the witch to feed her pets, or 'familiars' as they were known. The familiars were fed on their owner's blood.

The knowledge that some people had also led to suspicion. If they knew about herbal remedies, they were suspected of witchcraft. The people accused often lived alone and many were older women.

Anne Boleyn, King Henry VIII's second wife, was thought to be plotting to overthrow him and she was executed for this; but some people thought she was also a witch. She was even known to carry a sign of her witchcraft, as she had six fingers on one hand. (Actually, she only had the usual five fingers, but a wart on one of them gave people an excuse to accuse her.)

Testing for witchcraft

'Tests' were undertaken when an accusation was made. If a person reported that someone had 'bewitched' them, that was enough to trigger an investigation. There was no need to find evidence in order to accuse people of witchcraft. Look at the accusation in **Source B**.

Source B

The accusation made against Elizabeth Francis

In 1565, Elizabeth Francis confessed…that she had learned the art of witchcraft from her grandmother, who had given her a white spotted cat called Satan.

Elizabeth wanted a flock of sheep, and the cat 'in a strange hollow voice' promised she should have them. It brought her the sheep but they later disappeared.

Elizabeth was anxious to be married to Andrew Byles, who had previously 'abused' her. He refused to marry her so she ordered the cat to bewitch him and he died.

When she found that she was pregnant, the cat gave her a herb to eat, which destroyed the child. She then married Mr Francis, and when their baby was 6 months old, Elizabeth ordered the cat to murder it.

Each time the cat did something for her, Elizabeth gave it a drop of her blood. She kept the cat for 16 years, and then gave it to a poor woman in the neighbourhood.

Activity

1 Read **Source B**.
  a Make a list of all the parts of this account that you think are untrue.
  b What evidence could people have used to support the accusation against Elizabeth Francis?
  c We highlighted the word 'confessed'. Why is this such an important word in this source?
  d Today a story like this would make the headlines. How might Elizabeth Francis's behaviour be explained today?

2 People in the towns and villages of seventeenth-century England are looking out for witches, but they need help in spotting them. Design an eye-catching leaflet called 'How to spot a witch' to show what the telltale signs are. It will need a sketch of a typical witch and some details of the tests that could be used. To make it accessible to people in the seventeenth century it should have few words.

Topic 7   Was England cursed by evil?

Why were there so many witches?

Starter activity
How many signs are there that the people in the chairs are witches? Think about the different signs that were used.

Between 1600 and 1720 there was a frenzy of witch trials. It is estimated that around 1,000 people were executed for being a witch during this period.

Why did people in England become witch-crazy? To answer this we need to look at some surprising clues.

The 'Witchfinder General'

Clue 1
It was not uncommon for people to talk of 'popery' when they were talking about magic and witchcraft, as if the Catholic Church was connected with the problem in some way.

Clue 2
Elizabeth I introduced stronger laws against witches 5 years after becoming queen. She was keen to stop any problem of magic, especially while the country was under the threat of Spanish invasion.

Clue 3
King James I was so determined to show that witches were everywhere that he wrote a guidebook to help his subjects find them. In 1604 the law courts were allowed to try witches. The penalty was to be death.

Clue 4
Accusations of witchcraft came most commonly from neighbours.

Clue 5
There were more witch trials than usual during the Civil War (1642–49).

Clue 6
Witch trials reduced dramatically after Charles II was restored to the throne.

Clue 7
At the height of the Civil War, in 1645–46, a lawyer named Matthew Hopkins proclaimed himself the 'Witchfinder General', and earned his money by travelling around the country finding witches.

Clue 8
Most of Matthew Hopkins's witches were women over the age of 50.

Clue 9
Most of the women tried for witchcraft lived alone.

Clue 10
Burning at the stake was traditionally a punishment for heretics.

Clue 11
Some areas of England had more witches than others. Nearly 300 women were accused of witchcraft in Essex.

Clue 12
Some 'witches' found guilty in England served a prison sentence of 1 year, while others were executed.

Clue 13
Witch trials involved the suspect being bound hand and foot before the rope was wrapped around the waist. The accused was dunked in water (usually the village pond) to see if he/she floated or sank. If the accused floated, he or she was obviously a witch possessing magical power to survive the ordeal. If the accused sank, he or she was innocent. Sadly, many of those who sank drowned. They were innocent, but they died in proving it.

Clue 14
Puritans (extreme Protestants) ruled the country at this time. They were keen to clamp down on anyone who did not live a 'godly' life.

Clue 15
Matthew Hopkins was paid for each witch that he found.

Activity

1. You should now be able to add to your 'How to spot a witch' leaflet. Give details about the way a witch trial should be conducted. This could be in the form of a comic strip.

2. Why was it so difficult to prove that you were innocent of the crime of witchcraft in the seventeenth century?

3. You should now have some ideas about why there were so many witches in the seventeenth century. To help you refine your thinking, sort the clues into categories. Make a list of the clues that are to do with:
   a religious ideas
   b people's fears and suspicions
   c superstitions
   d individuals influencing others' decisions
   e any other category that you think could be important

4. Read the following statements:
   a 'People were living in turbulent and difficult times, and they could not understand the massive changes that were happening in their lives. They were keen to find someone to blame their worries on and they turned on "witches".'
   b 'People were encouraged by their rulers to be afraid of witches and to seek them out. This stopped them thinking about other big problems that the country faced.'
   c 'Many people in the seventeenth century genuinely believed that witchcraft existed and that the devil could control people's souls.'

   Try to find evidence from the clues to show how each of these statements *could be* correct.

5. In your opinion, why were there so many witches in seventeenth-century England?

Topic 8
Were plague and fire a disaster for London?

Why did the plague spread so quickly?

In an epidemic, a lot of people contract a disease at the same time and it spreads very quickly. In 1665, the inhabitants of London were struck by a killer epidemic that became known as the **Great Plague**. It was another outbreak of the disease medieval people feared so much that they named it the 'Black Death'.

In the earlier outbreaks of the disease, people had been convinced that it had been sent by God as a punishment 'for the wickedness of this time'. As a result, they prayed and whipped themselves in the hope of punishing themselves so that God would take the Black Death away. Might people in 1665 have reason to think that they had upset

The plague at its height in London

Activity

Look at the picture. What evidence is there that a terrible infectious disease is raging?

Using only the clues in the picture, explain why the plague spread so quickly.

God and that he had sent this punishment again? (Think about what had happened in England between 1640 and 1665).

Symptoms

The symptoms of the Great Plague were exactly the same as those from 300 years before. Medical knowledge had remained seemingly unchanged.

The disease usually began with a fever and quickly developed into sneezing and coughing. After that came sickness and vomiting. This was the most infectious phase of the disease.

Pink blotches appeared on the skin, and large swellings called **buboes** appeared in the groin and armpit. Shortly afterwards, the victim usually died. The whole process took between 3 and 5 days.

'Cures'

Many strange herbal cures were suggested, such as swallowing live toads — which is why people talk of having a 'frog in their throat' today. Others involved pigeons being split in half and held over a bubo to draw out its poison.

Some people believed that a gold coin in the mouth would ward off evil. Others carried a posy of sweet-smelling herbs at all times to combat the disease in the air.

Look at the picture in **Source A**. Despite his appearance, this was not a quack doctor. He was a qualified physician who was taking sensible precautions against contracting the plague.

Other problems

There were a number of other problems that the people of London had to struggle with as a result of the plague:

- There was a shortage of coffins.
- There was a shortage of graves.
- People still had to go about their daily lives, trading and working.
- Shops still had to stay open.
- Merchants and visitors still came to the city from outside.
- London's population was big, around 180,000 people.
- The buildings of London were all built very close together and overhung the streets.

Source A A plague doctor

- Heavy felt hat with a wide brim
- Beak: material stuffed with herbs or scented flowers
- Leather cowl covering the whole face, so that it is difficult for air to get in; glass beads where eyes should be
- Long frock coat: woollen cloth impregnated with wax to stop air getting in
- Large stick to fend off the crowds in the cramped streets
- Heavy leather gauntlets to protect the hands
- Breeches: worn under the coat and made of the same material
- Knee-length stiff leather boots, with breeches stuffed into the tops

Activity

What did people at the time think were the main causes of the plague? Try to work it out from **Source A**.

Topic 8   Were plague and fire a disaster for London?

Plague Town

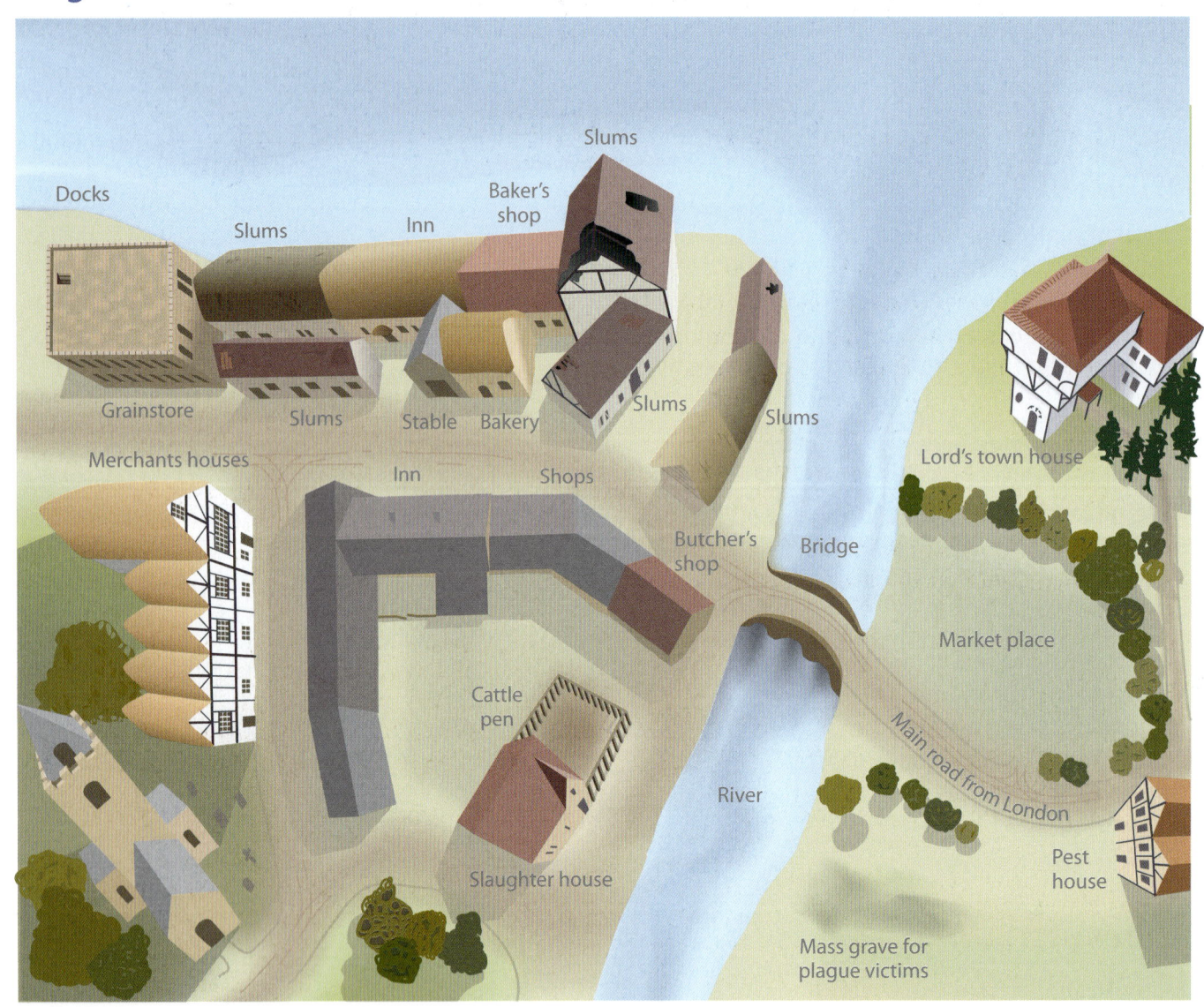

Labels on the map: Docks, Slums, Inn, Baker's shop, Slums, Grainstore, Slums, Stable, Bakery, Slums, Slums, Merchants houses, Inn, Shops, Butcher's shop, Bridge, Lord's town house, Market place, Cattle pen, River, Main road from London, Slaughter house, Mass grave for plague victims, Pest house

Activity

Look at the picture of Plague Town. Imagine you are in charge of stopping the plague from spreading further. You have the power to make any changes that you wish to solve the problems. You might find it easier to work with a partner.

1. Think about the ways that the disease might spread. What could you do to stop them?
2. What would you do with visitors to the town?
3. What would you do to secure the docks?
4. What would you do with the houses?
5. What problems might there be with other buildings and structures such as the stables, the church or the bridge?
6. What would you do about the problems that the people of London had to deal with? They would be a problem in Plague Town too.
7. Compare your solutions with the rest of the class. Be prepared to explain them.

What was done to stop the plague spreading?

There was a lack of medical knowledge about the real causes of the plague. We now know that it was caused by the fleas that lived on the back of the black rat. Humans were infected when they were bitten by those fleas. Because people did not know this, a lot of the measures that were put in place were futile.

Read the regulations in **Source A**, which were designed to stop the plague from spreading.

Activity

1 Read **Source A** and answer the following questions:
  a How do these measures compare with your own for Plague Town? What are the similarities and differences?
  b Would you adopt any of the Lord Mayor of London's rules to improve your plan for combating the spread of the plague?
  c Do you think that any of the Lord Mayor's rules would have helped control the spread of the disease in London? Explain your answer.
  d The jobs listed in Source A were dangerous and in some cases life-threatening. Which jobs would you find the hardest to do?
  e Write a job advertisement for one of the jobs that might tempt someone to do it.

Source A: The Lord Mayor of London's orders to stop the plague

1. Examiners:
To enquire what houses be visited by illness and what persons be sick, and of what diseases. And if they find any person sick of the infection the house shall be shut up for a month and none can leave the house. Every house infected to be marked with a red cross a foot long with these words 'Lord have mercy upon us'.

2. Searchers:
Women searchers to be appointed. They shall make a search and make a report whether the persons do die of the infection, or of what other diseases. No searcher be permitted to keep any shop or stall, or work as a laundress.

3. Watchmen:
For every infected house there be appointed watchmen, one for the day and one for the night. They have a special care that no person goes in or out of infected houses.

4. Householders:
Every householder must keep the street before his door swept all the week long.

5. Rakers and dog-killers:
The filth of the houses be daily carried away by the Rakers. No hogs, cats or rabbits to be kept in the city. Dogs to be killed by the dog-killers.

6. The burial of the dead must always be before sunrise or after sunset. No friend can accompany the corpse to church on pain of having his house shut up. All the graves shall be at least six feet deep.

Adapted from Shephard, C. et al. (2001) *Rediscovering the Making of the U.K.*

Topic 8 — Were plague and fire a disaster for London?

Source B A picture from a pamphlet published during the plague, illustrating the Lord Mayor's rules

Activity

1. Look at **Source B**.
   a Find people in the picture doing five jobs described in Source A.
   b Using Source B as a guide, illustrate some of your rules for Plague Town.
2. Look at the causes of the plague or its spread, and some of the effects of the plague. **Causes** are things that make other things happen. **Effects** are the result of things that have happened.
   a Divide the facts into the causes and the effects of the plague and write them in two separate lists in your exercise book.
   b Decide which are the **three most important causes**, and explain why they are important.
   c Decide which are the **three most important effects** of the plague, and explain why they are important.
   d Was it possible for the plague to return to London? If it did return, would it spread so quickly and kill so many people? Explain your answer.

Causes and effects of the plague

10 The plague had been a regular visitor for many years. There was little medical knowledge about it and nobody had managed to find a cure.

1 People blamed foreigners for the plague, as they thought it had come from abroad.

2 The plague had claimed 80,000 lives when it finally subsided in late summer 1666.

9 There were a larger number of quack cures at the end of the Great Plague than at the beginning.

3 Filth and human waste were found in the streets. There was no proper drainage and nowhere to bury the dead bodies.

8 The major symptoms of bubonic plague are:
- large buboes (swellings in the groin and armpits)
- flu-like symptoms
- sweating
- sneezing
- vomiting
- a large red rash

4 London's buildings were very close together. Many overhung the streets.

5 London's buildings were made from wooden frames, with walls of wattle and daub (sticks woven together and covered with a kind of mud), and were an ideal place for fleas to live. They remained in the same condition afterwards.

7 London's streets, with their open sewers, were the ideal breeding ground for rats, fleas, bacteria and disease. They remained the same after the plague subsided.

6 Fleas that lived on the back of black rats were the cause of bubonic plague, but this was not discovered for a number of years. Medical knowledge did not improve as a result of the Great Plague.

Topic 8 Were plague and fire a disaster for London?

Was the Great Fire of London a disaster?

Many people in England felt that their actions had been judged by God. They had seen religion become extreme with the Puritans. They had seen a monarch lose a war against his own people and then lose his head. They had lived through a military dictatorship and had even seen Christmas banned.

People thought that things would improve when Charles II was restored to the throne. However, they had not reckoned with the plague, which devastated London in 1665, killing 80,000 people.

Yet their torment was still not over. In 1666, a huge disaster came hard on the plague's heels. London was ravaged by fire.

London's burning

Thomas Farriner was a baker. As usual, he was awake in the early hours of 2 September 1666, stoking his oven to bake his bread. He went back to bed to wait for the oven to reach the right temperature, but when he awoke, it was to the smell of burning.

Farriner's house on Pudding Lane was on fire. He managed to escape, along with his wife and daughter, but the fire was already raging out of control.

The devastation

In the 4 hours between 3 a.m. and 7 a.m. the fire destroyed many houses. Panic began to sweep through London. The fire burned for another 5 days, and the devastation it brought was spectacular.

By the time the fire was put out on 7 September, 13,000 houses had been destroyed, leaving many thousands homeless.

Activity

The Great Fire of London: causes and consequences

Causes	Consequences
The houses in London were made of wood, and they overhung the streets…	…but people were keen to stop their houses being destroyed and often waited too long.
The summer of 1665 had been hot and dry…	…and as a result, the fire-fighters had very little water to fight the fires with.
People thronged the streets, trying to escape the flames;…	…so people built tall houses that were squashed together.
Houses were pulled down in an attempt to make a fire-break so that the flames had nothing left to spread to…	…which caused the flames to be blown from one building to another.
London Bridge had the main pump for getting water from the Thames, but it was one of the first things to be burned down…	…but this made it difficult for the fire-fighters to get to the blazing buildings, and held up the job of putting the flames out.
There was a strong easterly wind that blew for 3 days…	…so the attempts to stop the blaze were haphazard.
The cost of land in London was high because a lot of people wanted to live there…	…so the timbers in the walls of the houses were as dry as tinder.
There were no properly trained fire-fighters and no continuous supplies of water…	…so they would burn very easily.

❶ Copy the table into your exercise book and match up the causes and consequences of the Great Fire of London.

❷ a Colour-code your table. Use three different colours to mark the problems that were caused by:
   - natural causes
   - lack of technology
   - human error
   b Which problems tell us why the fire could not be stopped?
   c Which problems tell us why the fire was bound to spread?

❸ Look at the picture below. It is an artist's impression of what London looked like after the fire. What improvements appear to have been made?

Eighty churches, including St Paul's Cathedral, had also been destroyed.

The death toll was not huge, as most people were able to see the fire coming, blown on by the east wind. They had time to get away from the flames, but they could not save their property. One of the main reasons for this was that London had had a very dry summer, and water levels were not as high as usual. To make matters worse, the Lord Mayor had no real plan in place to fight a fire on this scale.

The 'new' London after the fire

Topic 8 — Were plague and fire a disaster for London?

Who was to blame?

Some people in London were convinced that the Great Fire was the work of foreign agents who were trying to destroy England. They even put a Frenchman, Robert Hubert, on trial for starting the blaze. He was found guilty and hung, even though he was not in the country at the time of the fire.

The opportunity for a new city

The destruction of London was nearly complete. Seventy-five percent of the city was destroyed. However, instead of seeing it as a disaster, it offered a once-in-a-lifetime opportunity for the citizens of London. They could rebuild the city from scratch and plan out the streets and buildings.

Some of the **costs** and **benefits** of the fire are shown in **Source A**.

a I'm upset because it will cost a lot of money to rebuild the city.

b The streets are much nicer places to walk in now.

c I have a chance to design exactly what I need.

d I'll have to pay more money to safeguard my house.

e The government has started to stick its nose into my business, telling me what I can and can't build with.

f I'm safe from the plague in this clean city.

g I can't just build what I want, where I want.

Insurance man

Architect

Activity

1 Sort the statements in **Source A** into costs and benefits.

2 The comments below were made by:
  a a London architect
  b a citizen of London
  c an insurance company representative
Look at the statements and match them with the correct speaker.

3 How would the newspapers of the time have dealt with this story? Would they have written a positive or negative account of the fire and its consequences? Write a headline that sums up what has happened to London as a result of the fire.

Source A

Costs and benefits of the Great Fire of London

1. The great St Paul's Cathedral was burned to the ground.
2. 13,000 private houses were lost. They were replaced by 9,000 new houses.
3. People were able to rebuild their houses in the same places as before.
4. Wood was used less as a building material as it was seen as being unsuitable after the fire.
5. Brick was readily available for building.
6. Stone became more expensive as a building material.
7. Laws were passed about what sorts of buildings should be put up.
8. Houses could not be more than 35 feet high.
9. Streets were replanned so that they were not as cramped and close together.
10. Sunlight could reach the new streets.
11. There were more cobbled streets, from which the filth might drain away quicker.
12. Insurance companies sprang up. They offered fire insurance to home owners in case their houses burned down.
13. Insurance companies started to train and equip their own fire-fighting teams so that they could stop fires from getting out of hand.
14. The fire killed many of the rats in London and destroyed the filthy houses that they lived in.
15. There was no serious outbreak of the plague in London after 1666.
16. Talented and visionary architects, like Sir Christopher Wren, had the chance to plan the new city.

j The city will be much safer now.

i There's an emergency service to help me in case of a fire.

Citizen

h I'll only deal with fires in properties that my business is responsible for.

Topic 9
Was there a revolution in England, 1500–1750?

What happened in England between 1500 and 1750?

We are now going to sum up the period that our book covers. Look at the timeline which shows all the things that happened during the reigns of the monarchs we have looked at. Read through it carefully to get an overview of those times and answer the questions in the Activity box.

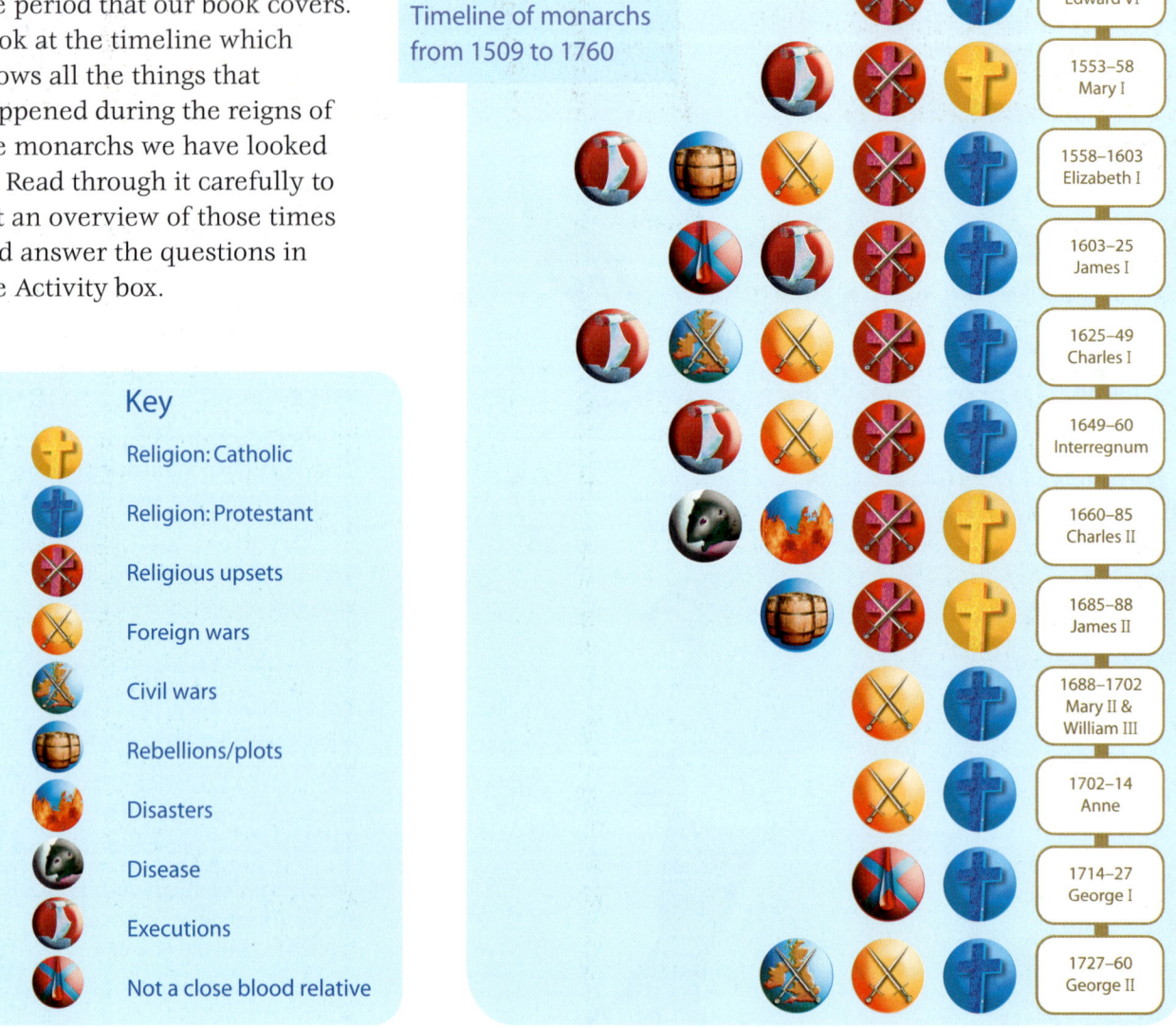

Timeline of monarchs from 1509 to 1760

1509–47	Henry VIII
1547–53	Edward VI
1553–58	Mary I
1558–1603	Elizabeth I
1603–25	James I
1625–49	Charles I
1649–60	Interregnum
1660–85	Charles II
1685–88	James II
1688–1702	Mary II & William III
1702–14	Anne
1714–27	George I
1727–60	George II

Key
- Religion: Catholic
- Religion: Protestant
- Religious upsets
- Foreign wars
- Civil wars
- Rebellions/plots
- Disasters
- Disease
- Executions
- Not a close blood relative

Activity

1. How long is a century?
2. In what century was 1547?
3. How many kings ruled between 1509 and 1760?
4. How many queens ruled between 1509 and 1760?
5. How many kings ruled in the seventeenth century?
6. How many kings are shown as ruling in the sixteenth century?
7. Which king ruled for the longest period?
8. Which queen ruled for the longest period?
9. Which monarch had the shortest reign?
10. How many monarchs used executions?
11. How many monarchs fought foreign wars?
12. How many monarchs fought civil wars?
13. How many monarchs faced religious difficulties?
14. How many monarchs fought off plots?
15. How many monarchs took the throne even though they were not closely related to the previous king or queen?
16. What is the approximate average length of rule of kings?
17. What is the approximate average length of rule of queens?
18. In which century were there least religious problems?
19. How many Protestant monarchs were there from 1509 to 1760?
20. Why was there an 'interregnum'? Choose the **best** answer.
    a. Because there was no one left to be king.
    b. Nobody wanted to be king.
    c. It is the name of a king.
    d. The previous king was executed.
21. Which sentence **best sums up** the period 1509–1760?
    a. It was a time of great upheaval for all the rulers of England.
    b. It was a period in which Parliament wrested power from the monarchy.
    c. It was a period in which Protestant monarchs finally ruled the country.
    d. It was a time when religious problems became less important.
22. Use the timeline to set five more questions for your neighbour to answer.

Topic 9 — Was there a revolution in England, 1500–1750

Activity

Look at the list of topics. It contains all the elements of a 2-hour documentary that you should imagine you are going to make about the period 1500–1750.

1. Decide how much time you would give to each element in your programme. It all has to fit into the 2 hours, so for each element, you need to suggest how many minutes it will get.

   Hint: you don't have to include all the elements in the documentary, but if you leave things out you will need to explain why.

2. Copy the circles (right) and divide them up to show how many minutes you have given each element.

3. Would you make this documentary in chronological order or not? Explain your decision.

4. Write a brief paragraph explaining why each element has been given the amount of time allocated. Which elements will be the most important?

5. Write a brief description of the points you want to make for each element. Remember that you want to give the viewer an overview of the whole period.

How much time should you spend on each topic?

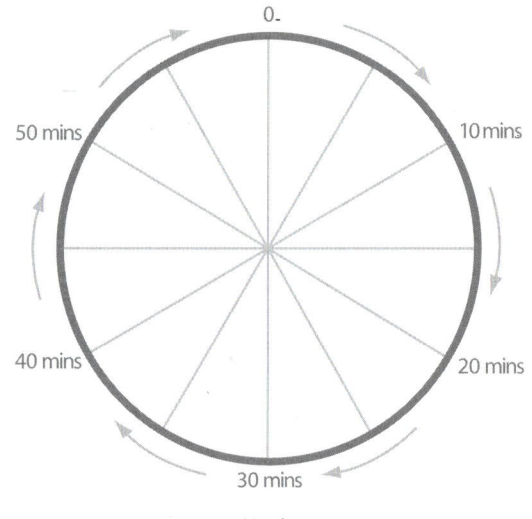

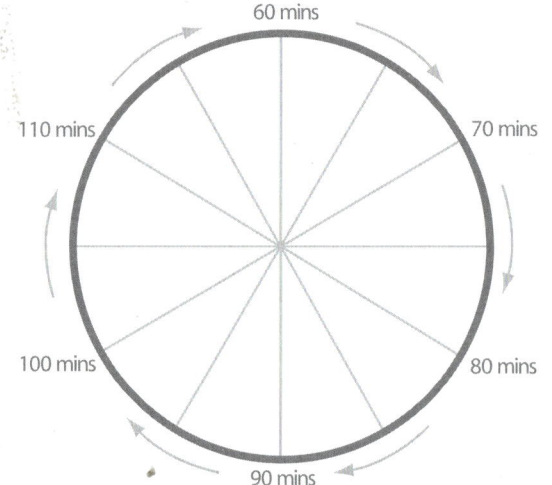

Circle 1: 0, 10 mins, 20 mins, 30 mins, 40 mins, 50 mins

Circle 2: 60 mins, 70 mins, 80 mins, 90 mins, 100 mins, 110 mins

Activity

The front cover of this textbook was designed to give some clues about the content of the book and what we think is important in this period.

6. Design a new front cover for this book. Use as many images as you want. The main thing is to sum up the important parts of the book.

7. For your cover, think of a more imaginative title than 'The Making of the UK'. For instance, a good title for a book on the medieval realms might be 'Conquering kings and revolting peasants'. It captures a couple of big ideas and it sounds interesting.

Topics

Relations with Scotland
The role of the monarchy
The Interregnum
Disasters: the Great Plague
Disasters: the Great Fire of London
The power of Parliament
The Civil War
Causes of the Civil War
Relations with Ireland
Clashes with Parliament
Religious problems
Witchcraft